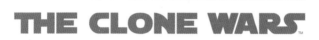

STAR WARS

THE CLONE WARS™

DEADLY HANDS OF SHON-JU

W9-BPP-548

DESIGNER **KRYSTAL HENNES**

ASSISTANT EDITOR **FREDDYE LINS**

EDITOR **RANDY STRADLEY**

PUBLISHER **MIKE RICHARDSON**

Special thanks to Jann Moorhead, David Anderman, Troy Alders, Leland Chee, Sue Rostoni, and Carol Roeder at Lucas Licensing.

Published by Dark Horse Books, a division of Dark Horse Comics, Inc.
10956 SE Main Street, Milwaukie, OR 97222

darkhorse.com | starwars.com

To find a comics shop in your area, call the Comic Shop Locator Service toll-free at 1.888.266.4226
First edition: December 2010 | ISBN 978-1-59582-545-2

10 9 8 7 6 5 4 3 2 1
PRINTED AT MIDAS PRINTING INTERNATIONAL, LTD., HUIZHOU, CHINA

STAR WARS: THE CLONE WARS—DEADLY HANDS OF SHON-JU

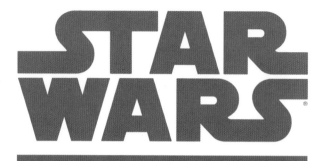

THE CLONE WARS

DEADLY HANDS OF SHON-JU

SCRIPT **JEREMY BARLOW**   ART **BRIAN KOSCHAK**

COLORS **RONDA PATTISON**   LETTERING **MICHAEL HEISLER**

COVER ART **SEAN MCNALLY**

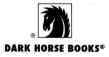

DARK HORSE BOOKS®

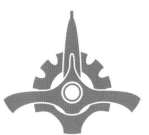

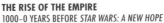

THE RISE OF THE EMPIRE
1000–0 YEARS BEFORE *STAR WARS: A NEW HOPE*

The events in these stories take place approximately twenty-two years before the Battle of Yavin.

After the seeming final defeat of the Sith, the Republic enters a state of complacency. In the waning years of the Republic, the Senate is rife with corruption, and the ambitious Senator Palpatine has himself elected Supreme Chancellor. This is the era of the prequel trilogy.

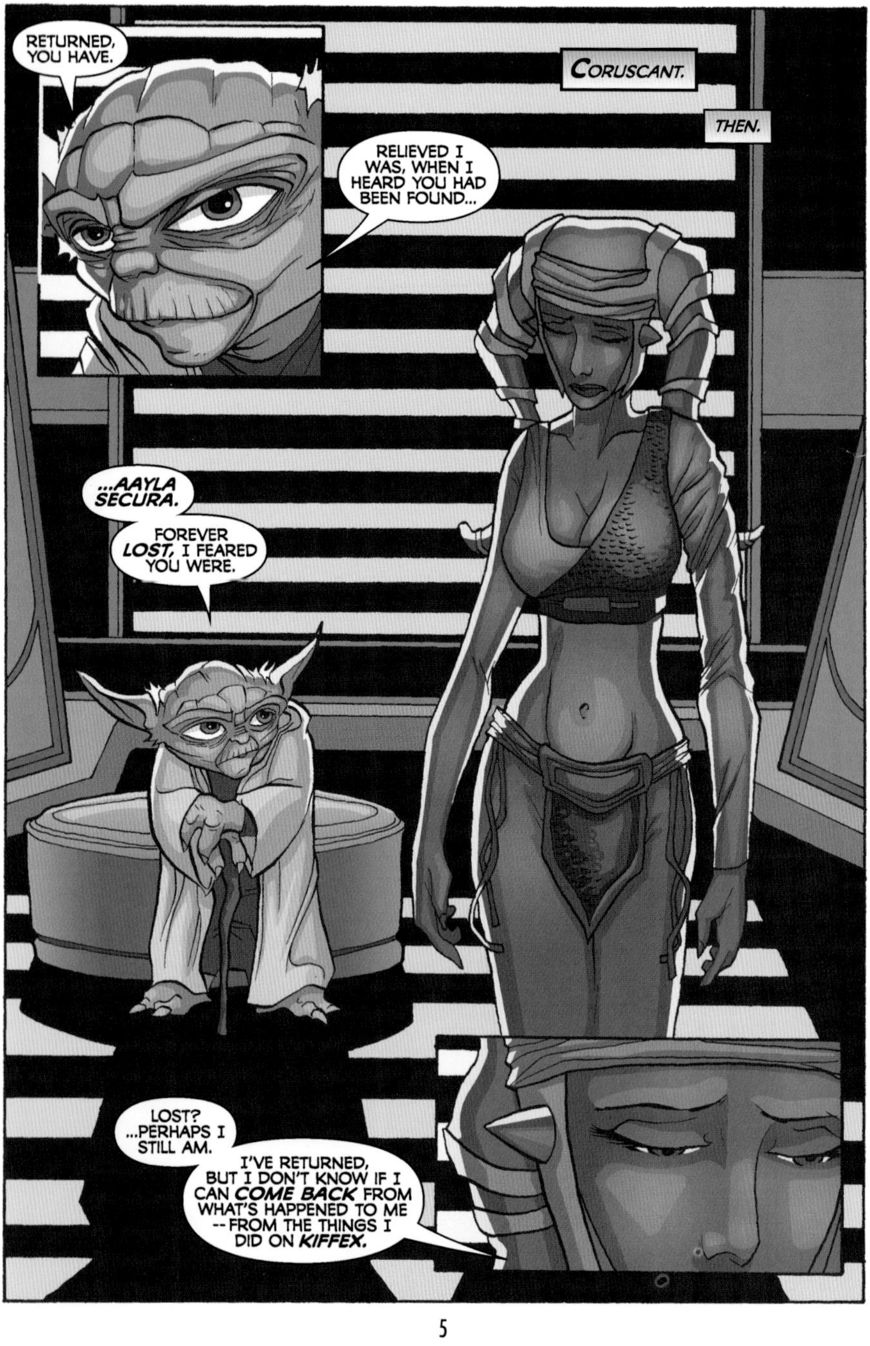
RETURNED, YOU HAVE.
CORUSCANT.
THEN.
RELIEVED I WAS, WHEN I HEARD YOU HAD BEEN FOUND...
...AAYLA SECURA.
FOREVER LOST, I FEARED YOU WERE.
LOST? ...PERHAPS I STILL AM.
I'VE RETURNED, BUT I DON'T KNOW IF I CAN COME BACK FROM WHAT'S HAPPENED TO ME --FROM THE THINGS I DID ON KIFFEX.

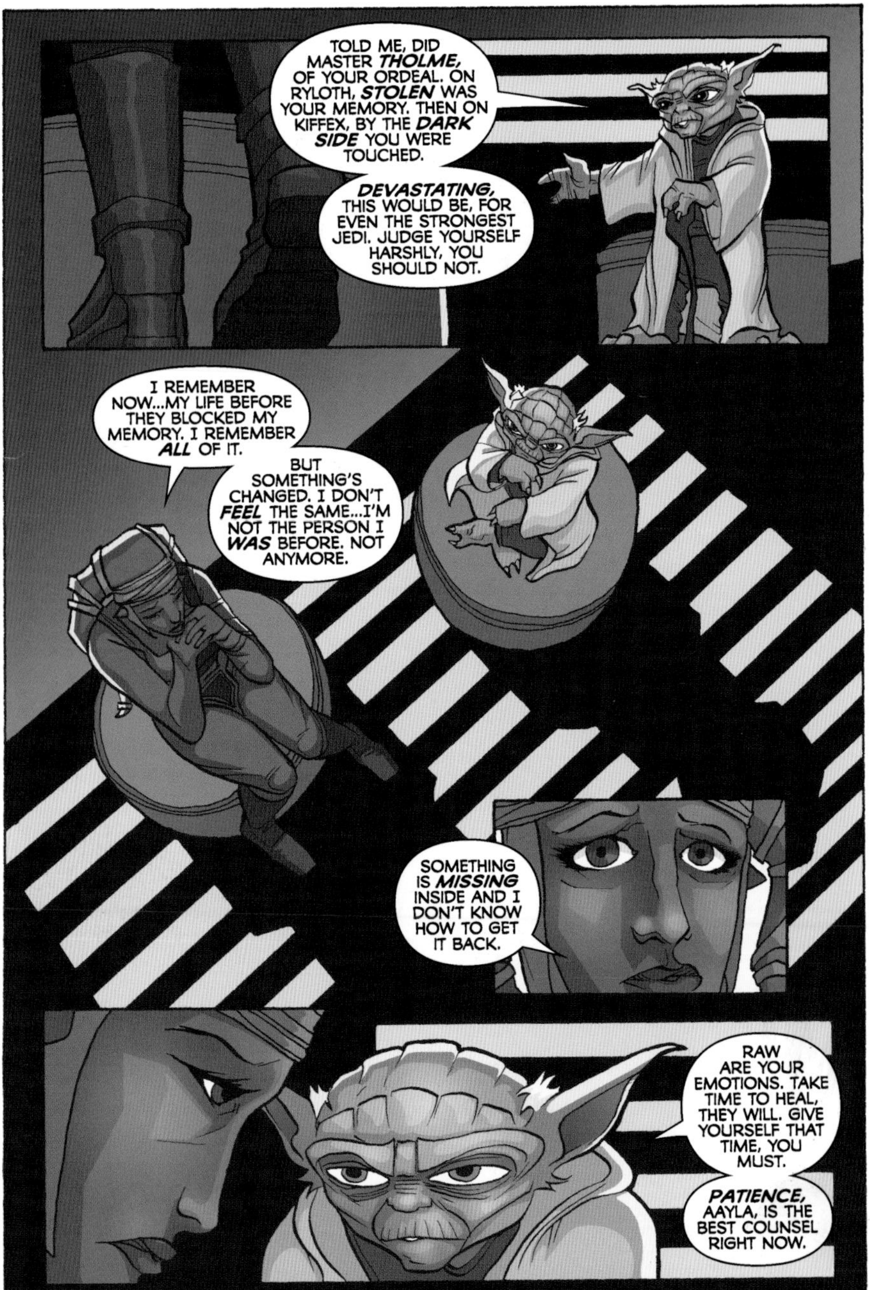
TOLD ME, DID MASTER THOLME, OF YOUR ORDEAL. ON RYLOTH, STOLEN WAS YOUR MEMORY. THEN ON KIFFEX, BY THE DARK SIDE YOU WERE TOUCHED.
DEVASTATING, THIS WOULD BE, FOR EVEN THE STRONGEST JEDI. JUDGE YOURSELF HARSHLY, YOU SHOULD NOT.
I REMEMBER NOW...MY LIFE BEFORE THEY BLOCKED MY MEMORY. I REMEMBER ALL OF IT.
BUT SOMETHING'S CHANGED. I DON'T FEEL THE SAME...I'M NOT THE PERSON I WAS BEFORE. NOT ANYMORE.
SOMETHING IS MISSING INSIDE AND I DON'T KNOW HOW TO GET IT BACK.
RAW ARE YOUR EMOTIONS. TAKE TIME TO HEAL, THEY WILL. GIVE YOURSELF THAT TIME, YOU MUST.
PATIENCE, AAYLA, IS THE BEST COUNSEL RIGHT NOW.

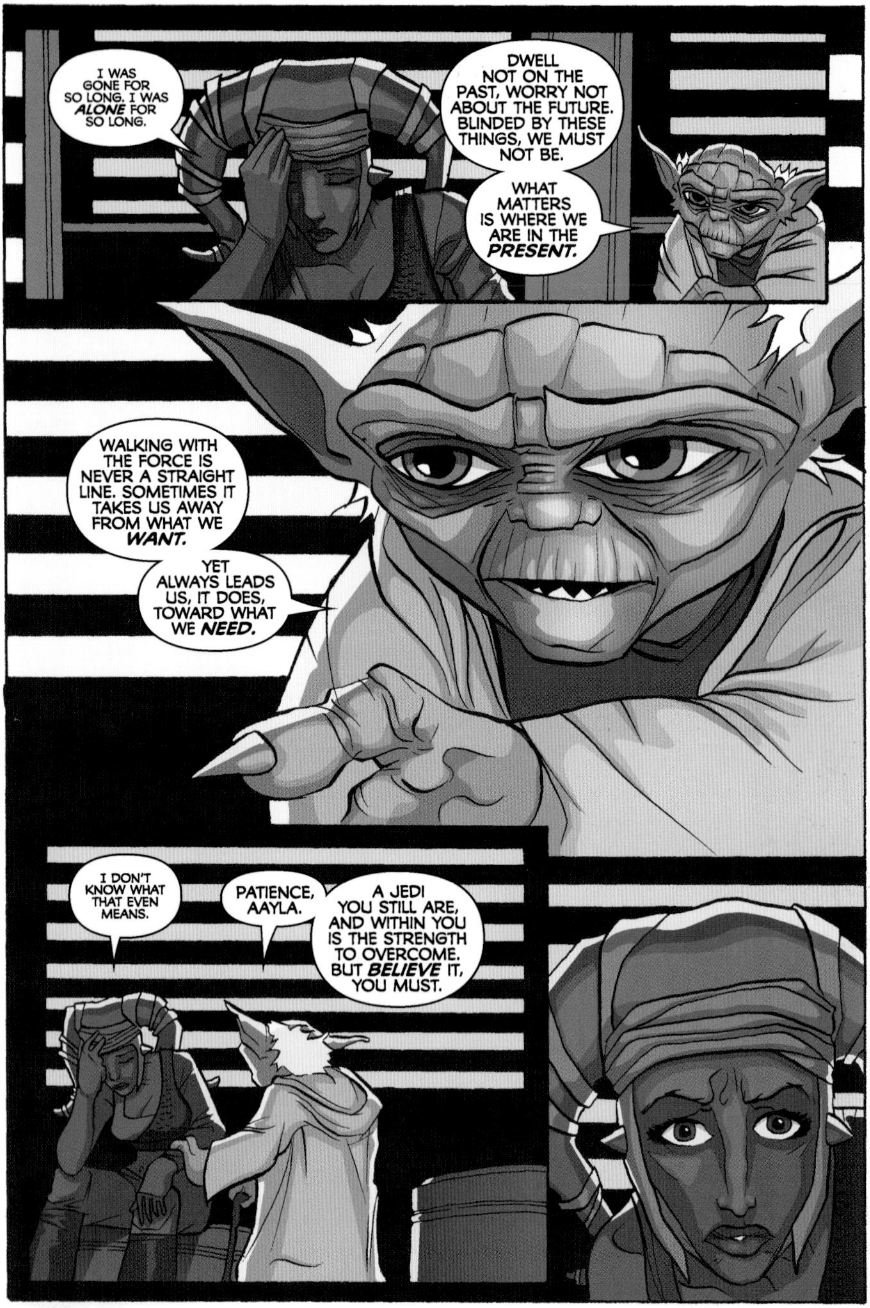
I WAS GONE FOR SO LONG. I WAS *ALONE* FOR SO LONG.
DWELL NOT ON THE PAST, WORRY NOT ABOUT THE FUTURE. BLINDED BY THESE THINGS, WE MUST NOT BE.
WHAT MATTERS IS WHERE WE ARE IN THE ***PRESENT.***
WALKING WITH THE FORCE IS NEVER A STRAIGHT LINE. SOMETIMES IT TAKES US AWAY FROM WHAT WE ***WANT.***
YET ALWAYS LEADS US, IT DOES, TOWARD WHAT WE ***NEED.***
I DON'T KNOW WHAT THAT EVEN MEANS.
PATIENCE, AAYLA.
A JEDI YOU STILL ARE, AND WITHIN YOU IS THE STRENGTH TO OVERCOME. BUT ***BELIEVE*** IT, YOU MUST.

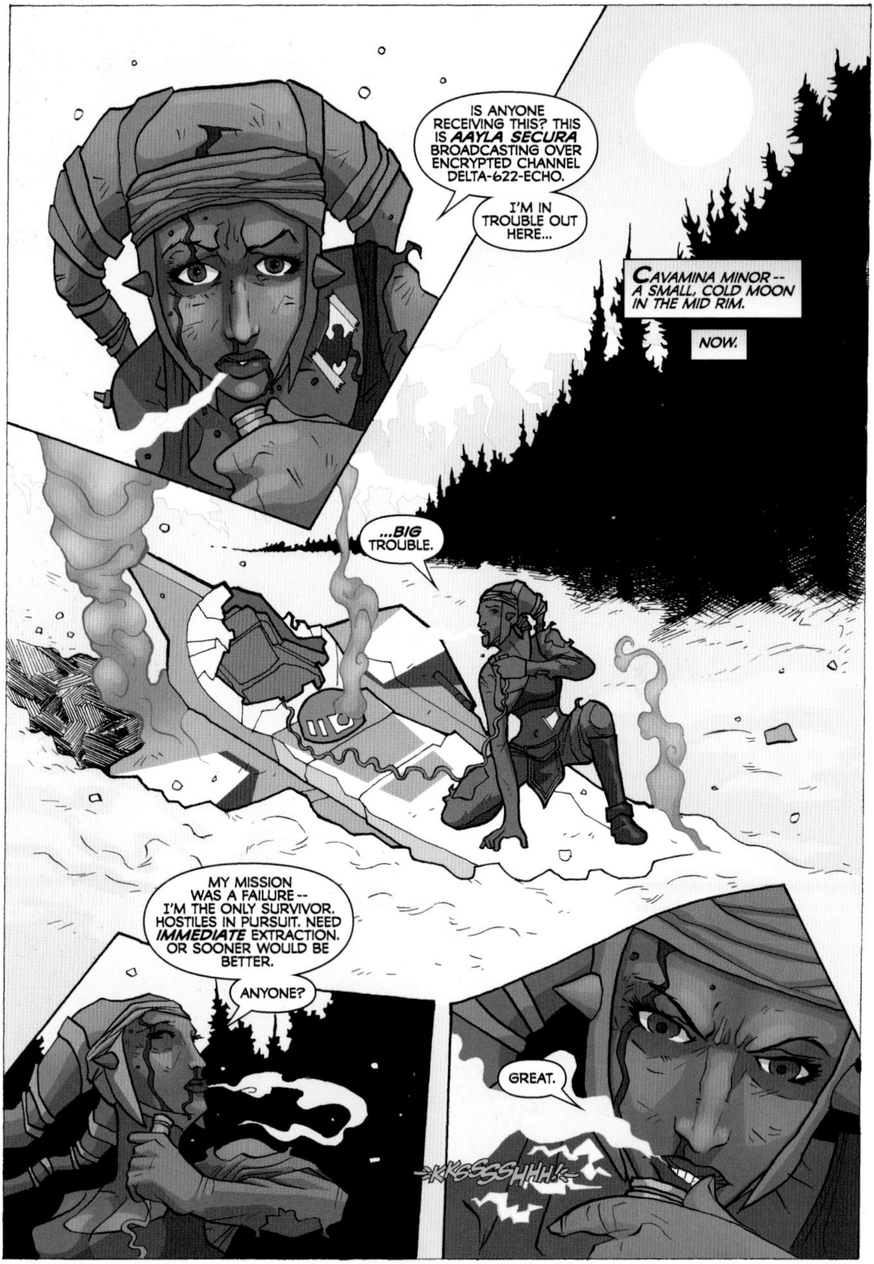
IS ANYONE RECEIVING THIS? THIS IS AAYLA SECURA BROADCASTING OVER ENCRYPTED CHANNEL DELTA-622-ECHO.
I'M IN TROUBLE OUT HERE...
CAVAMINA MINOR -- A SMALL, COLD MOON IN THE MID RIM.
NOW.
...BIG TROUBLE.
MY MISSION WAS A FAILURE -- I'M THE ONLY SURVIVOR. HOSTILES IN PURSUIT. NEED IMMEDIATE EXTRACTION. OR SOONER WOULD BE BETTER.
ANYONE?
GREAT.
KKSSSSHHH!

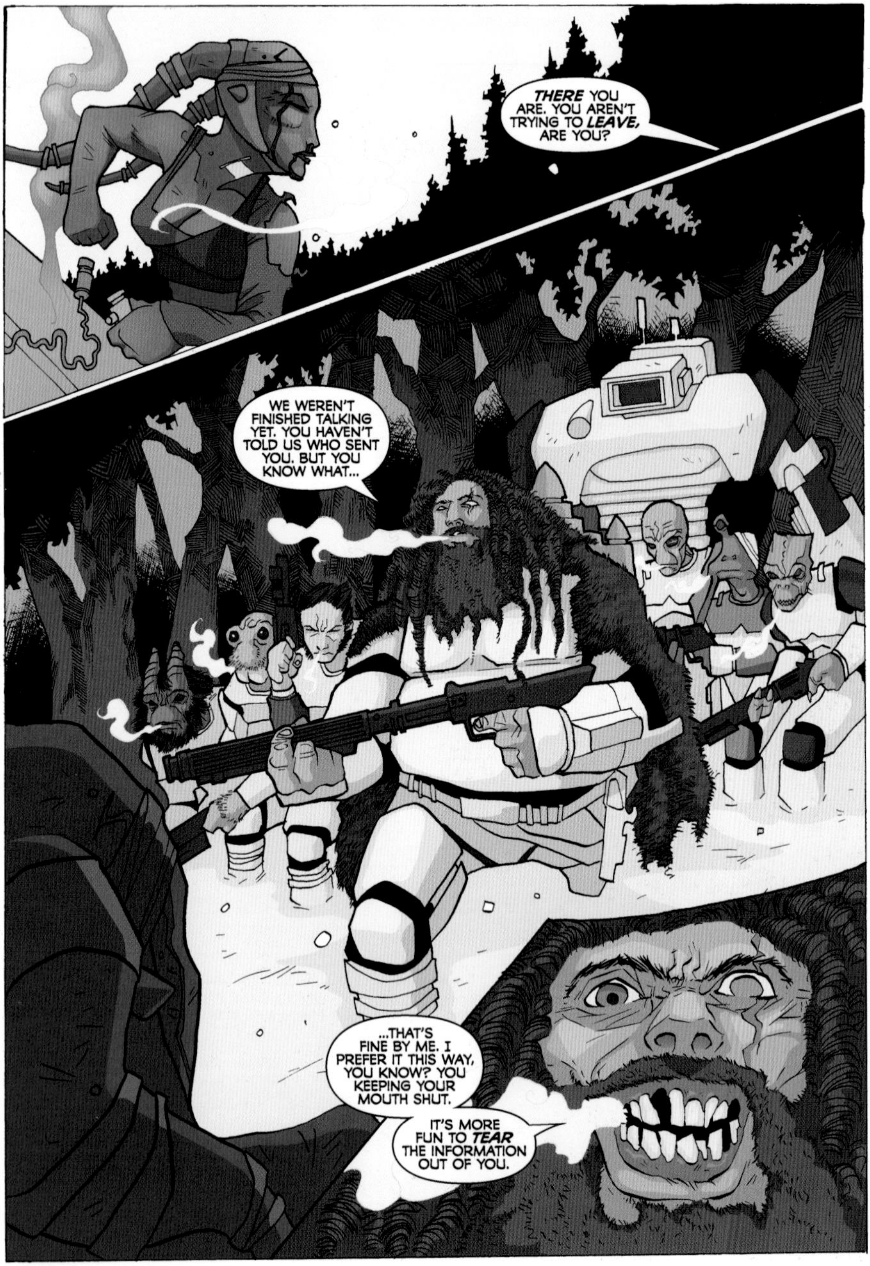
THERE YOU ARE. YOU AREN'T TRYING TO LEAVE, ARE YOU?
WE WEREN'T FINISHED TALKING YET. YOU HAVEN'T TOLD US WHO SENT YOU. BUT YOU KNOW WHAT...
...THAT'S FINE BY ME. I PREFER IT THIS WAY, YOU KNOW? YOU KEEPING YOUR MOUTH SHUT.
IT'S MORE FUN TO TEAR THE INFORMATION OUT OF YOU.

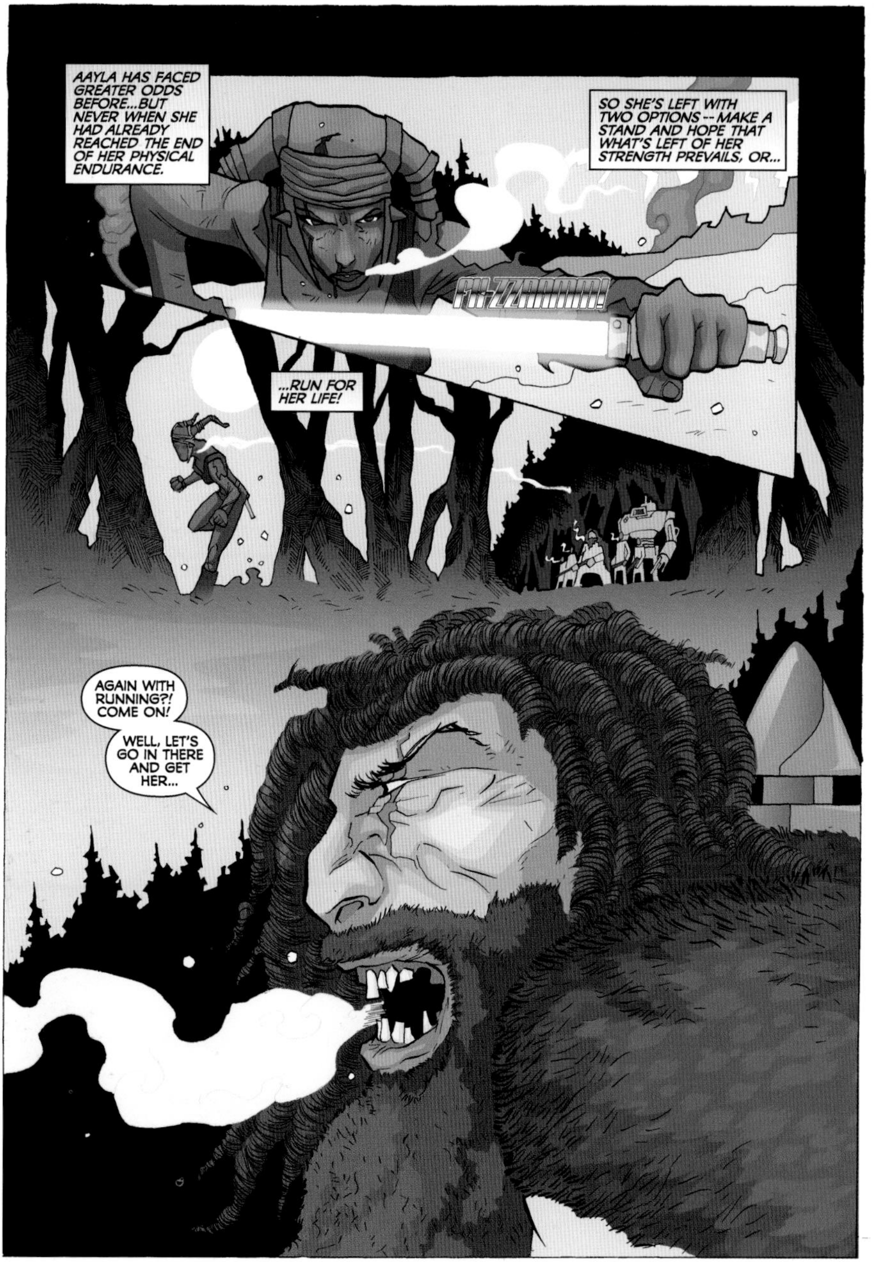
AAYLA HAS FACED GREATER ODDS BEFORE...BUT NEVER WHEN SHE HAD ALREADY REACHED THE END OF HER PHYSICAL ENDURANCE.
SO SHE'S LEFT WITH TWO OPTIONS -- MAKE A STAND AND HOPE THAT WHAT'S LEFT OF HER STRENGTH PREVAILS, OR...
...RUN FOR HER LIFE!
AGAIN WITH RUNNING?! COME ON!
WELL, LET'S GO IN THERE AND GET HER...

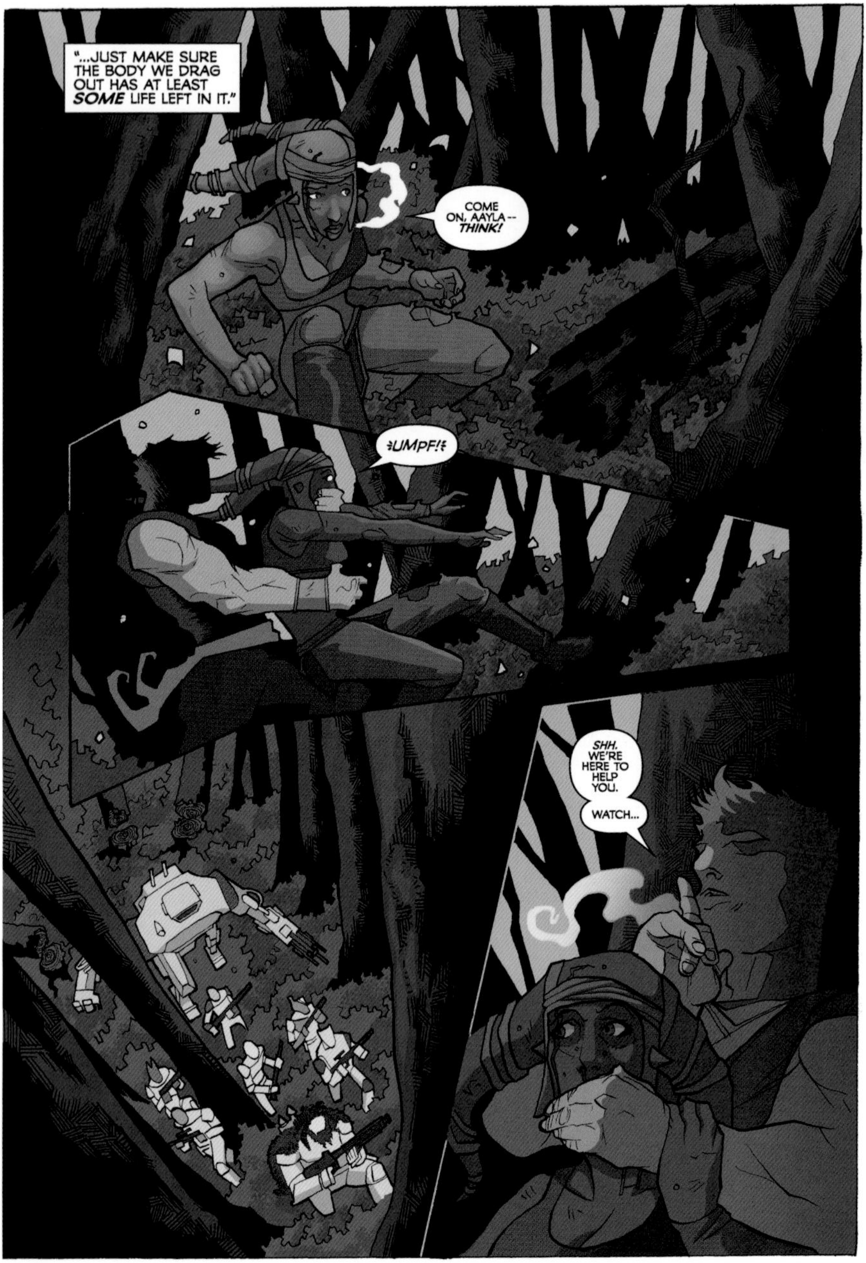
"...JUST MAKE SURE THE BODY WE DRAG OUT HAS AT LEAST *SOME* LIFE LEFT IN IT."
COME ON, AAYLA-- *THINK!*
UMPF!
SHH. WE'RE HERE TO HELP YOU.
WATCH...

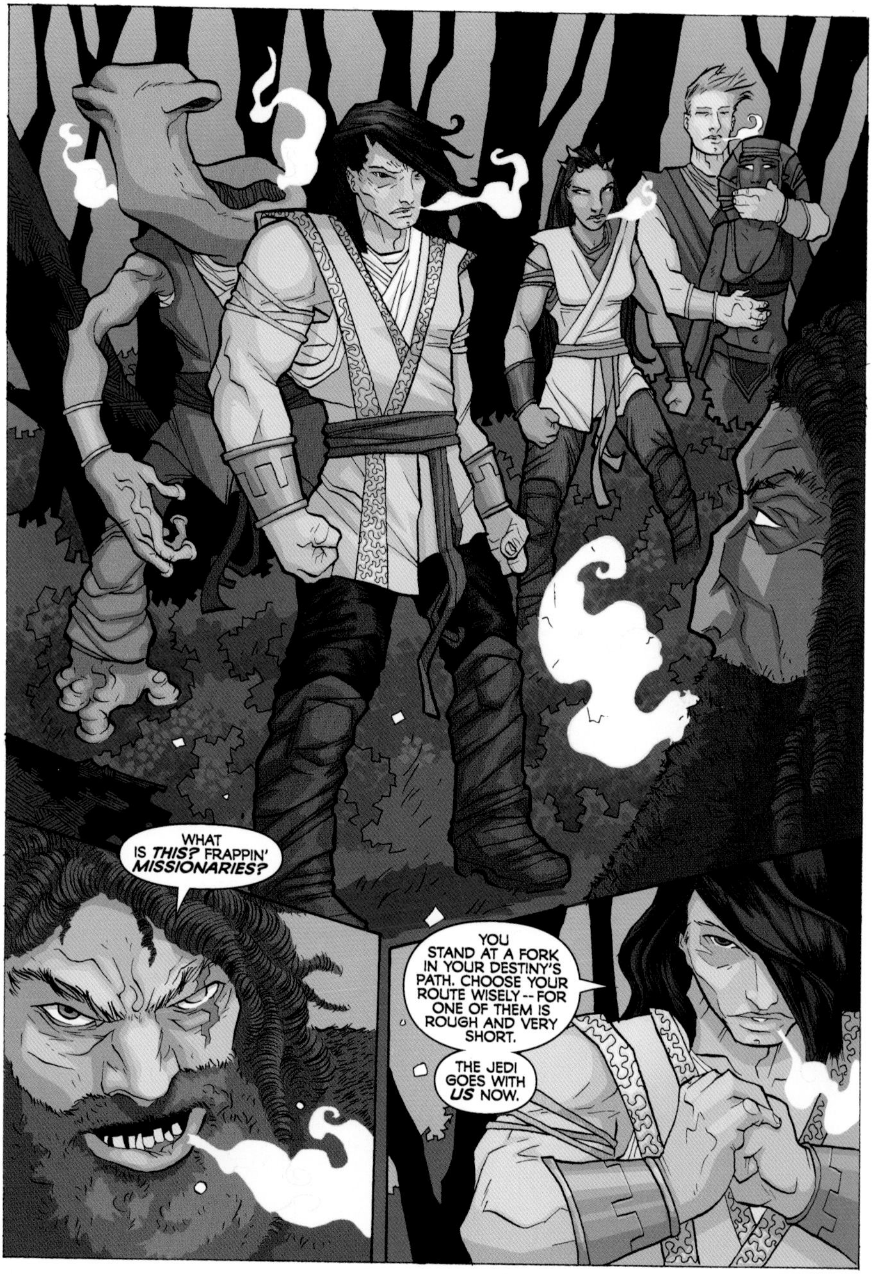
WHAT IS THIS? FRAPPIN' MISSIONARIES?
YOU STAND AT A FORK IN YOUR DESTINY'S PATH. CHOOSE YOUR ROUTE WISELY--FOR ONE OF THEM IS ROUGH AND VERY SHORT.
THE JEDI GOES WITH US NOW.

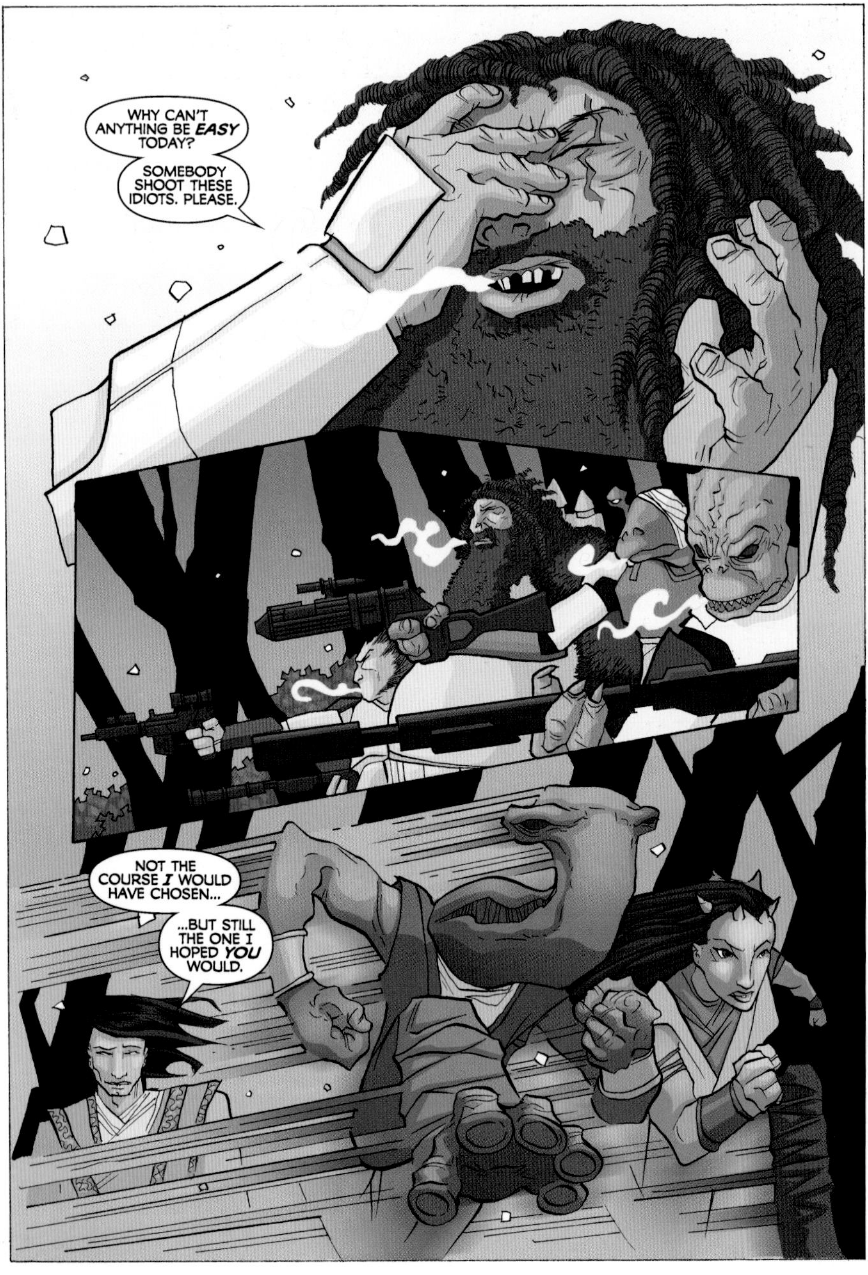
WHY CAN'T ANYTHING BE *EASY* TODAY?
SOMEBODY SHOOT THESE IDIOTS. PLEASE.
NOT THE COURSE *I* WOULD HAVE CHOSEN...
...BUT STILL THE ONE I HOPED *YOU* WOULD.

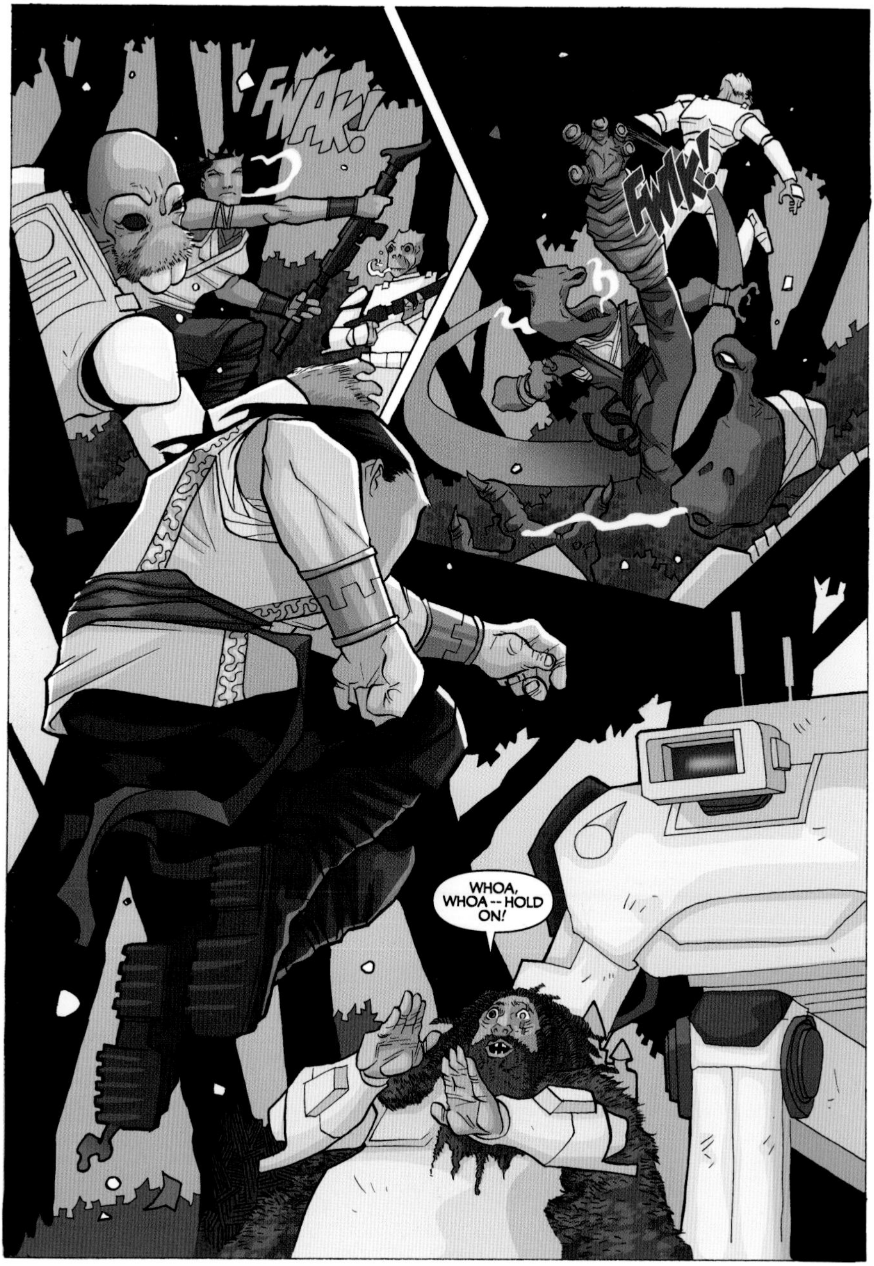
FWAK!
FWIK!
WHOA, WHOA--HOLD ON!

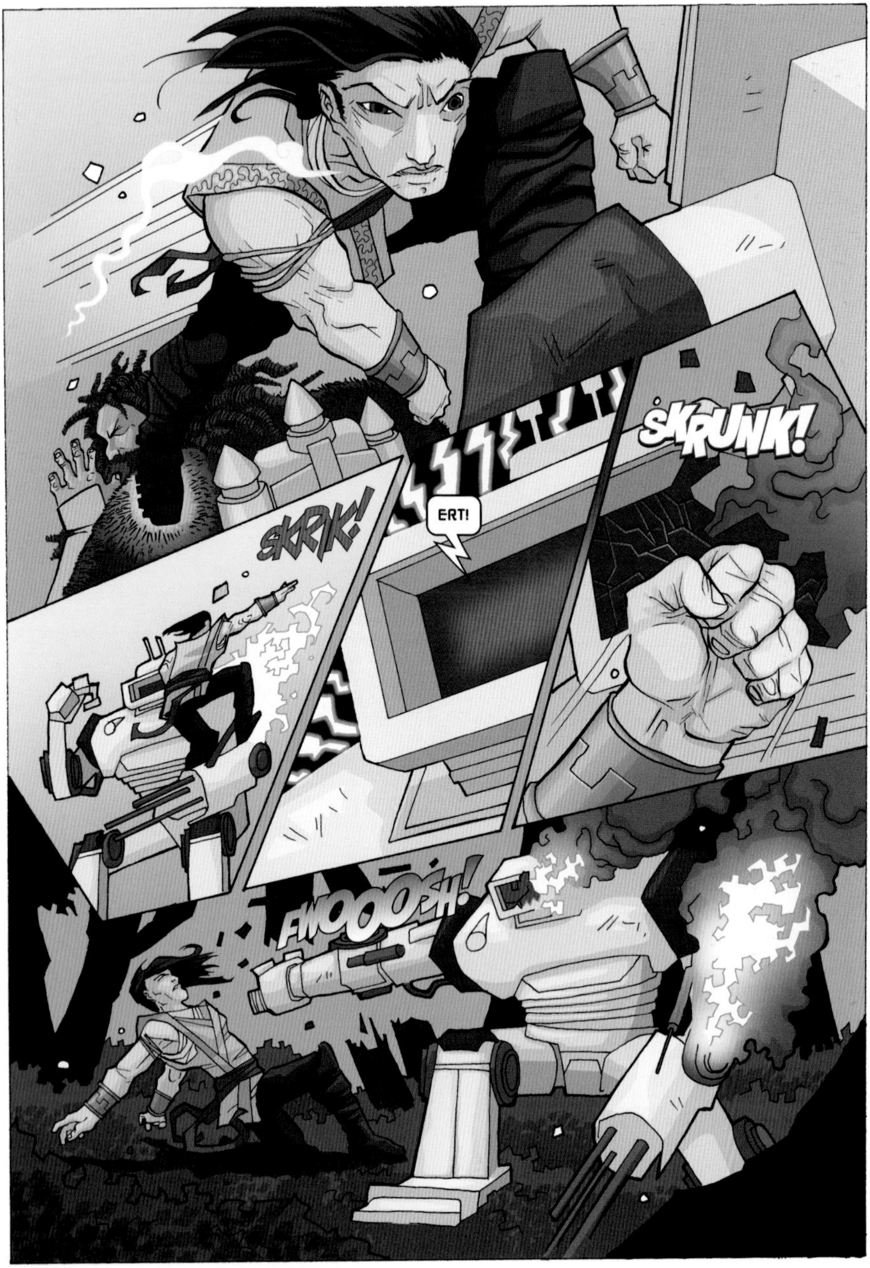
SKRIK!
ERT!
SKRUNK!
FWOOOOSH!

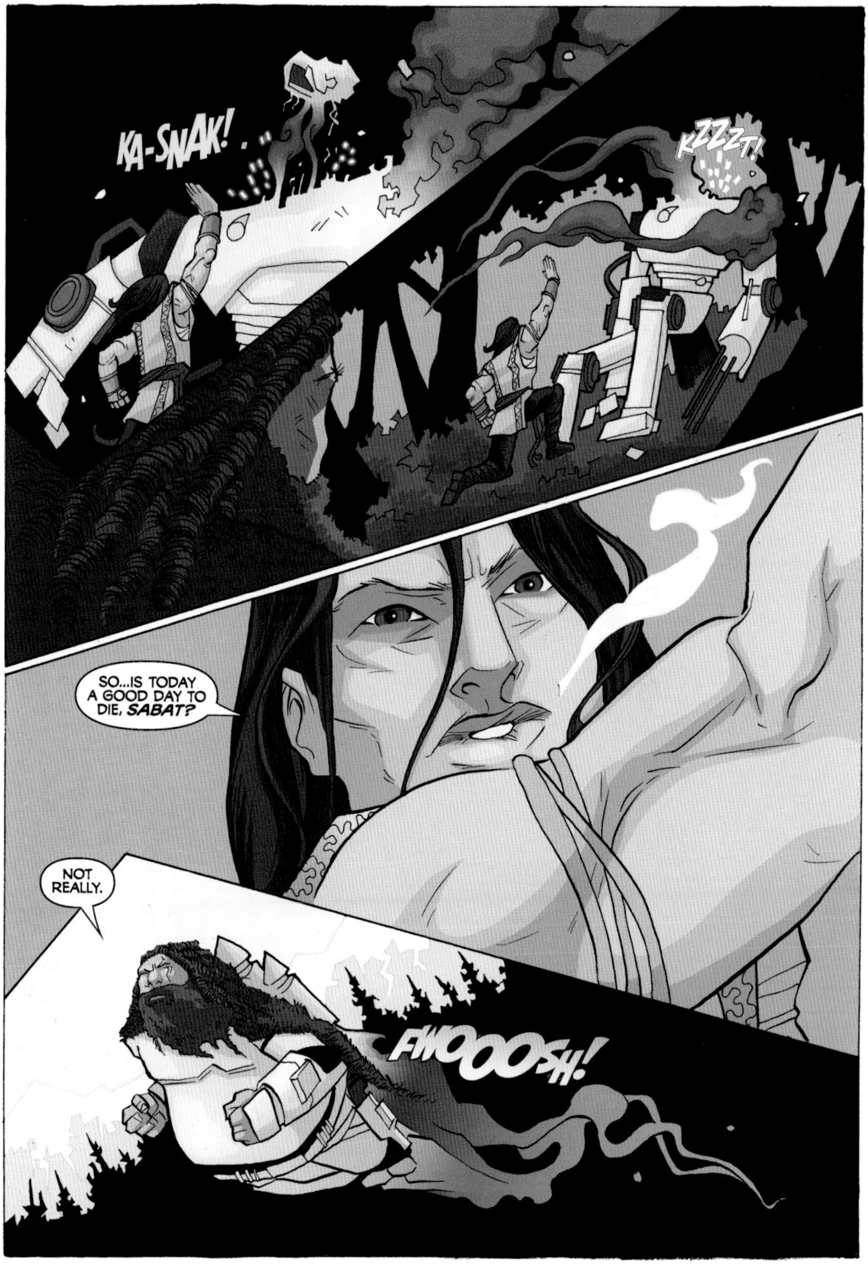
KA-SNAK!
KZZZT!
SO...IS TODAY A GOOD DAY TO DIE, SABAT?
NOT REALLY.
FWOOOSH!

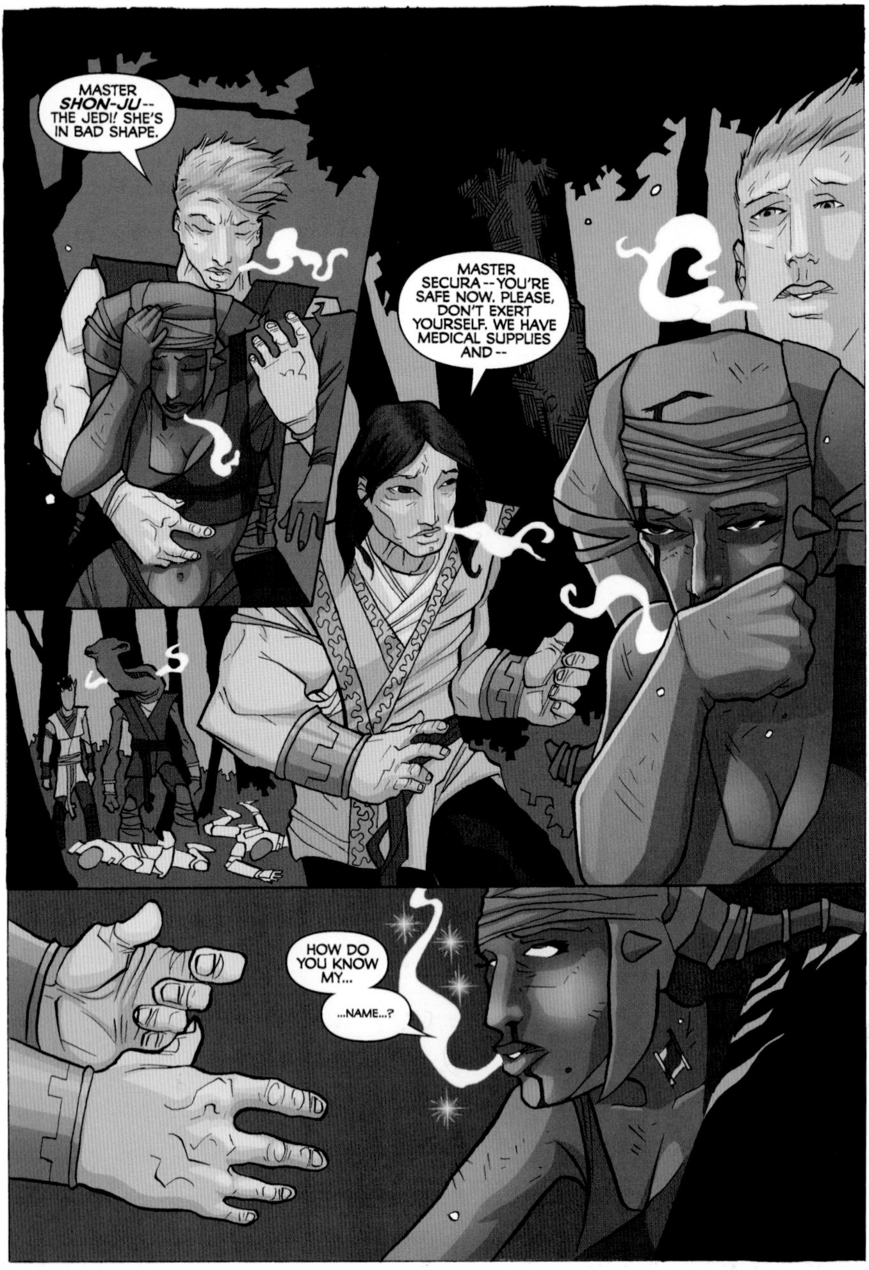
MASTER SHON-JU-- THE JEDI! SHE'S IN BAD SHAPE.
MASTER SECURA--YOU'RE SAFE NOW. PLEASE, DON'T EXERT YOURSELF. WE HAVE MEDICAL SUPPLIES AND--
HOW DO YOU KNOW MY...
...NAME...?

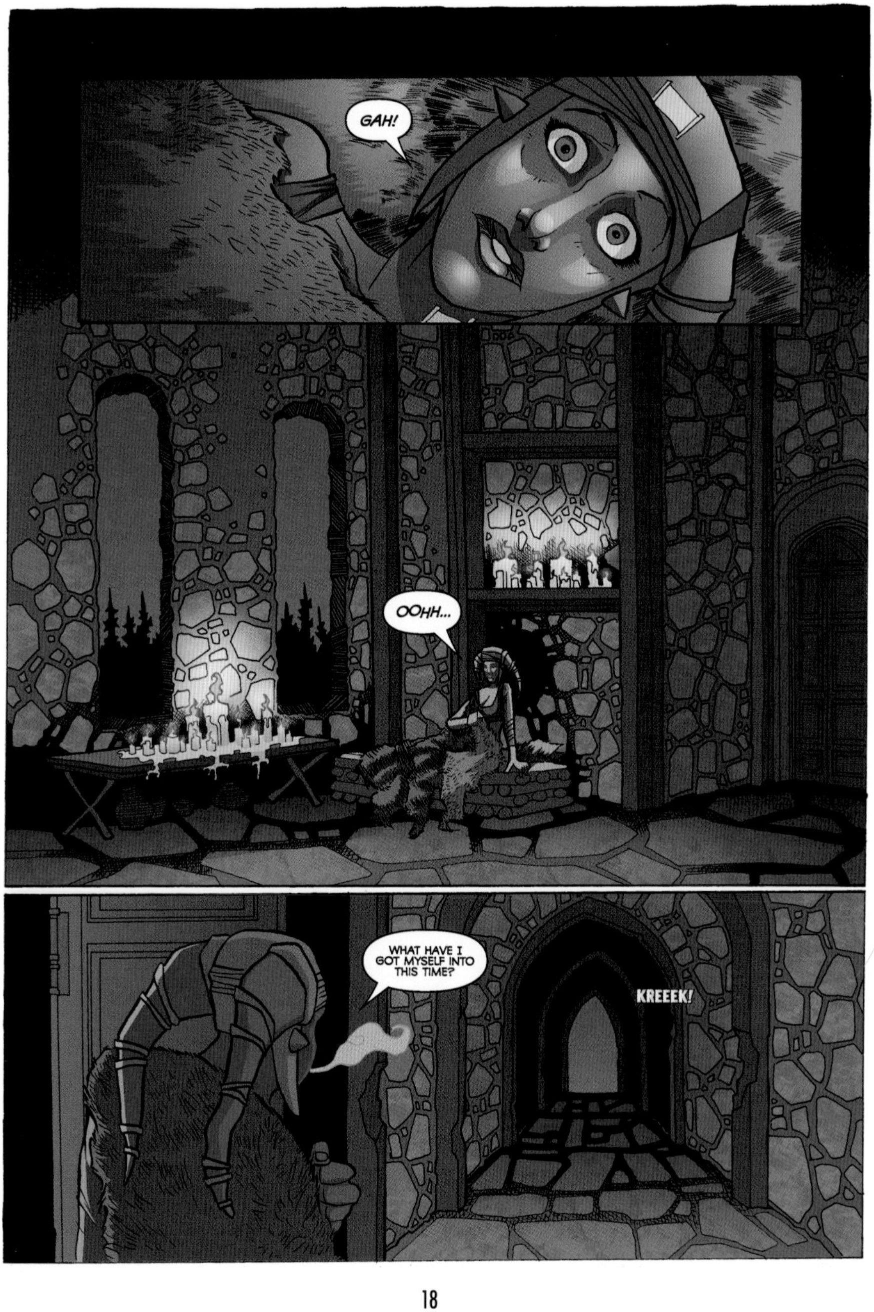
GAH!
OOHH...
WHAT HAVE I GOT MYSELF INTO THIS TIME?
KREEEK!

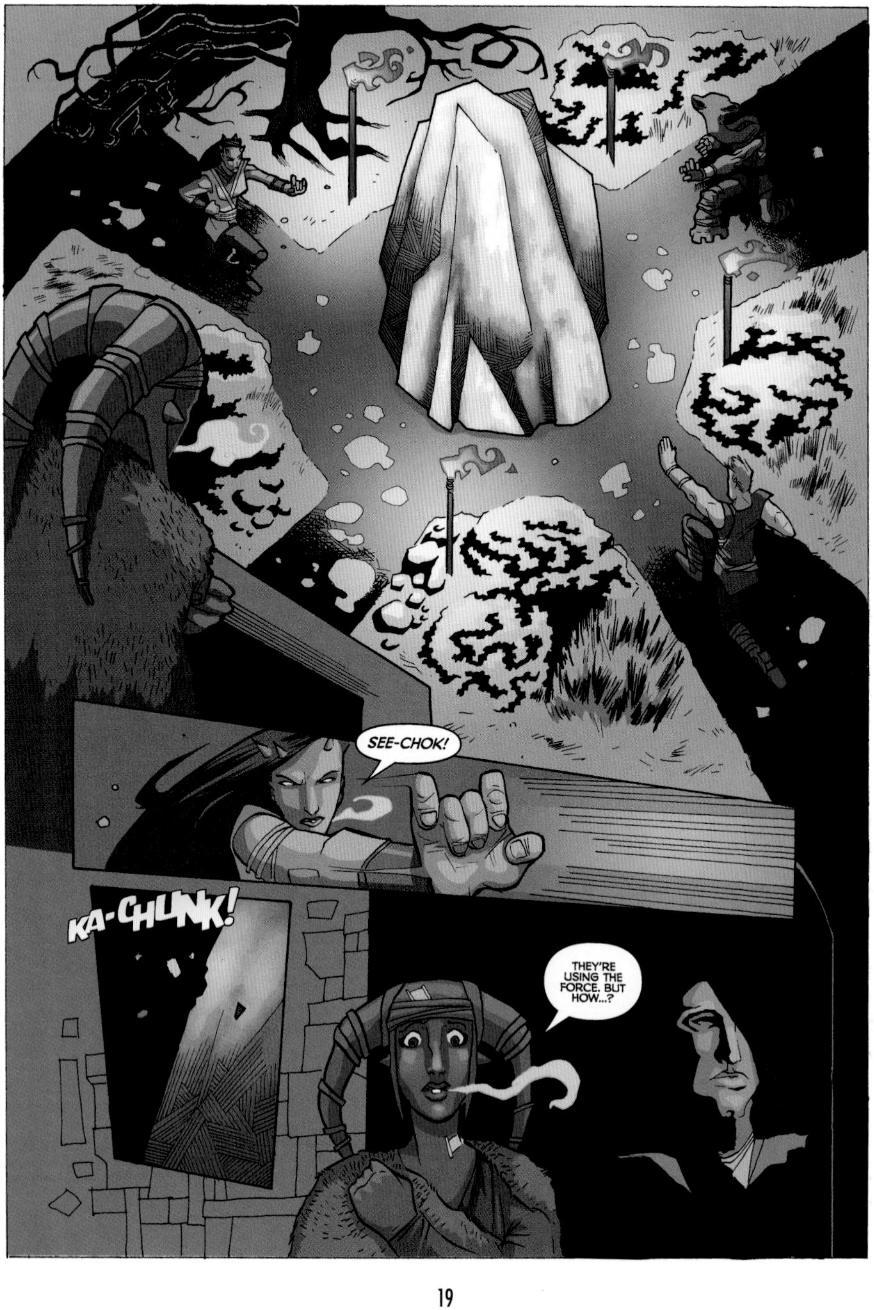
SEE-CHOK!
KA-CHUNK!
THEY'RE USING THE FORCE. BUT HOW...?

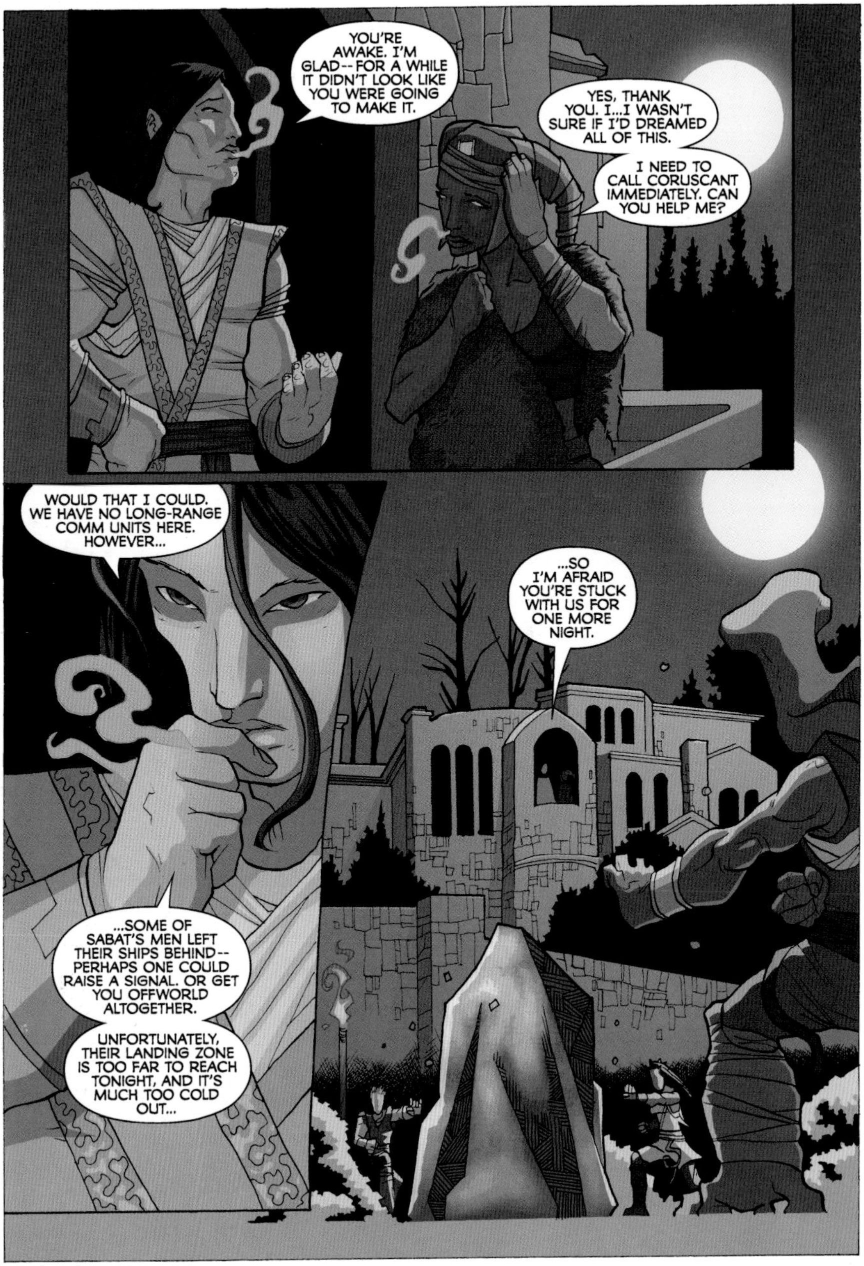
YOU'RE AWAKE. I'M GLAD-- FOR A WHILE IT DIDN'T LOOK LIKE YOU WERE GOING TO MAKE IT.
YES, THANK YOU. I...I WASN'T SURE IF I'D DREAMED ALL OF THIS.
I NEED TO CALL CORUSCANT IMMEDIATELY. CAN YOU HELP ME?
WOULD THAT I COULD. WE HAVE NO LONG-RANGE COMM UNITS HERE. HOWEVER...
...SOME OF SABAT'S MEN LEFT THEIR SHIPS BEHIND-- PERHAPS ONE COULD RAISE A SIGNAL. OR GET YOU OFFWORLD ALTOGETHER.
UNFORTUNATELY, THEIR LANDING ZONE IS TOO FAR TO REACH TONIGHT, AND IT'S MUCH TOO COLD OUT...
...SO I'M AFRAID YOU'RE STUCK WITH US FOR ONE MORE NIGHT.

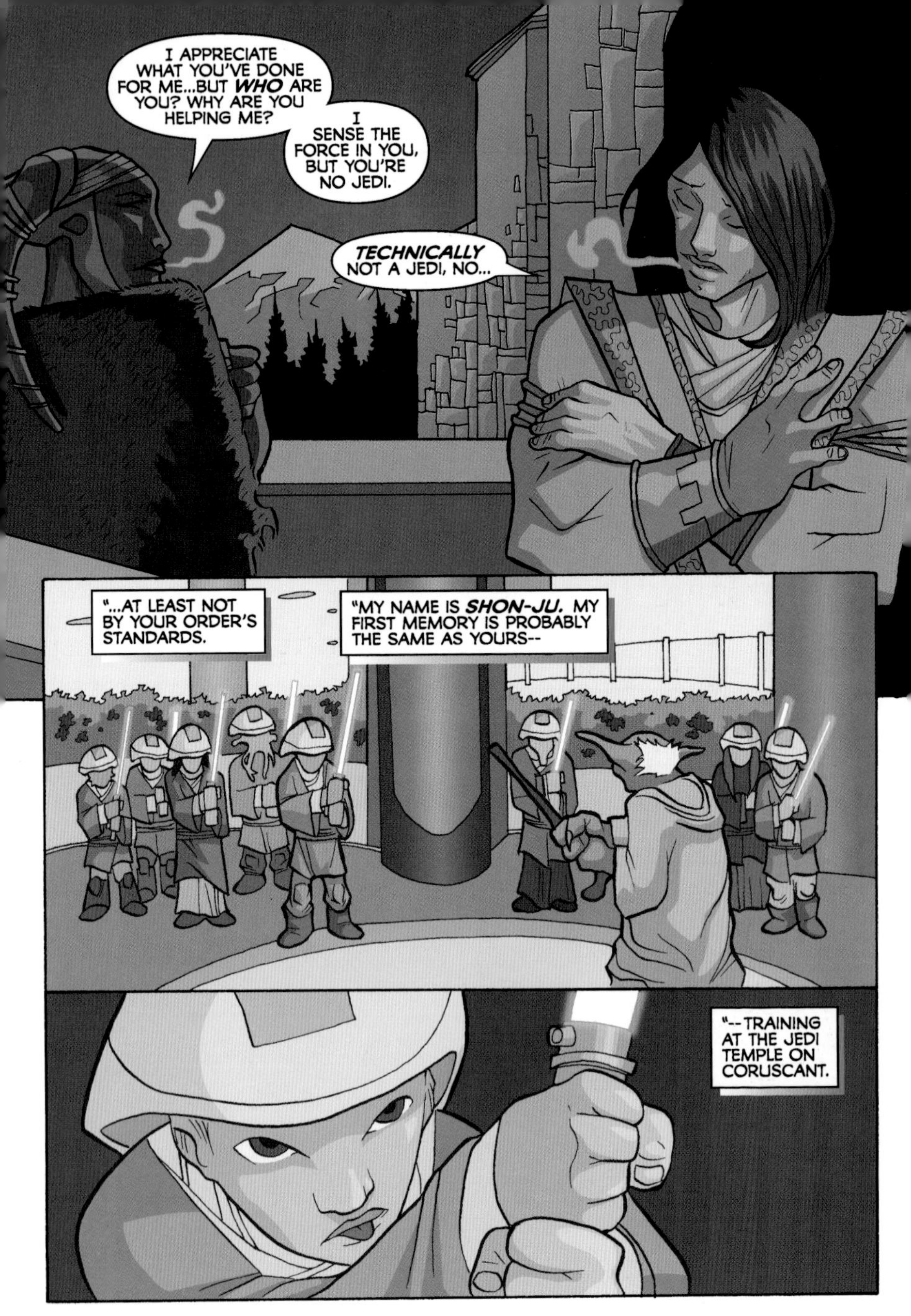
I APPRECIATE WHAT YOU'VE DONE FOR ME...BUT WHO ARE YOU? WHY ARE YOU HELPING ME?
I SENSE THE FORCE IN YOU, BUT YOU'RE NO JEDI.
TECHNICALLY NOT A JEDI, NO...
"...AT LEAST NOT BY YOUR ORDER'S STANDARDS.
"MY NAME IS SHON-JU. MY FIRST MEMORY IS PROBABLY THE SAME AS YOURS--
"--TRAINING AT THE JEDI TEMPLE ON CORUSCANT.

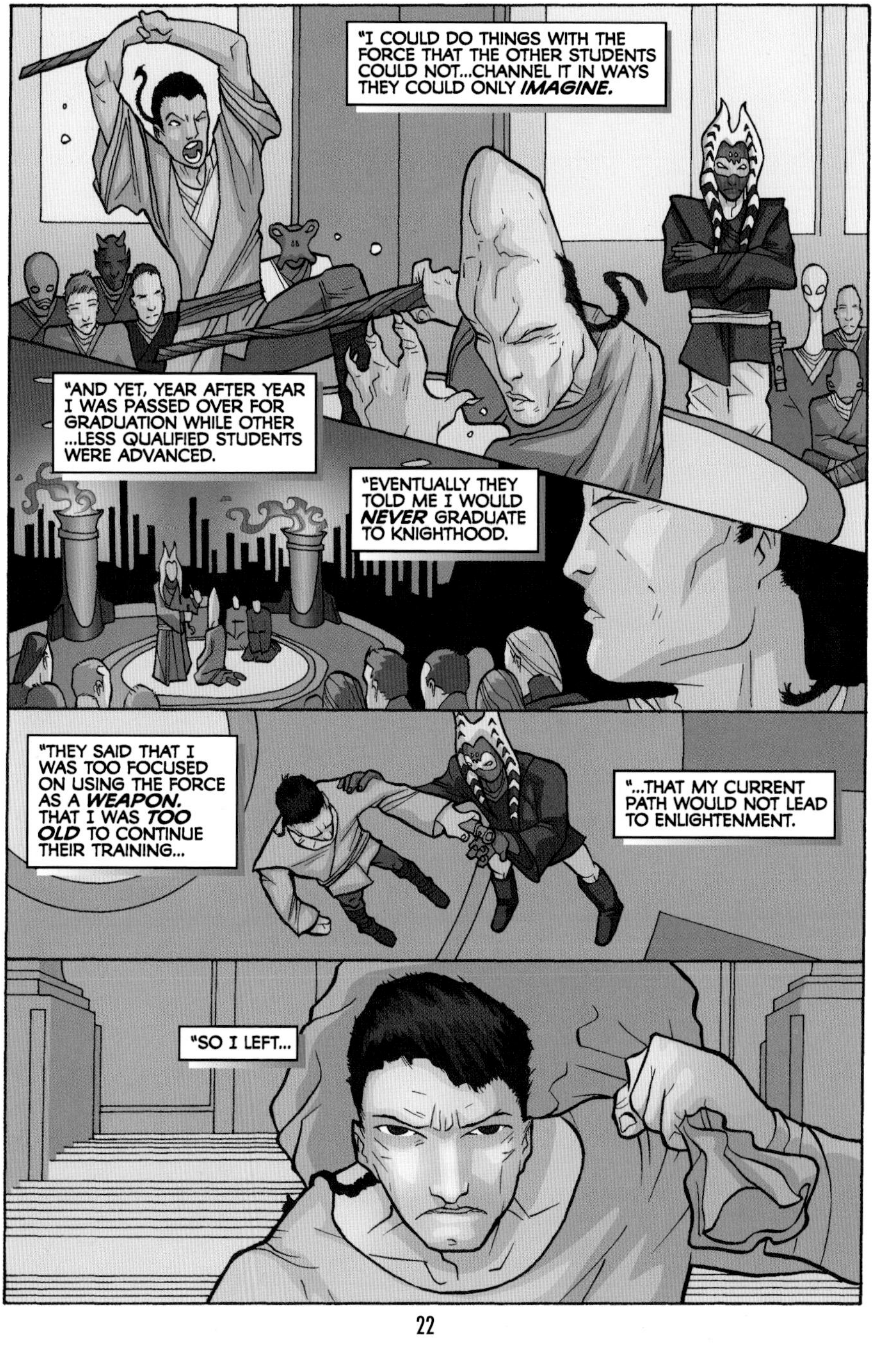
"I COULD DO THINGS WITH THE FORCE THAT THE OTHER STUDENTS COULD NOT...CHANNEL IT IN WAYS THEY COULD ONLY *IMAGINE.*
"AND YET, YEAR AFTER YEAR I WAS PASSED OVER FOR GRADUATION WHILE OTHER ...LESS QUALIFIED STUDENTS WERE ADVANCED.
"EVENTUALLY THEY TOLD ME I WOULD *NEVER* GRADUATE TO KNIGHTHOOD.
"THEY SAID THAT I WAS TOO FOCUSED ON USING THE FORCE AS A *WEAPON.* THAT I WAS *TOO OLD* TO CONTINUE THEIR TRAINING...
"...THAT MY CURRENT PATH WOULD NOT LEAD TO ENLIGHTENMENT.
"SO I LEFT...

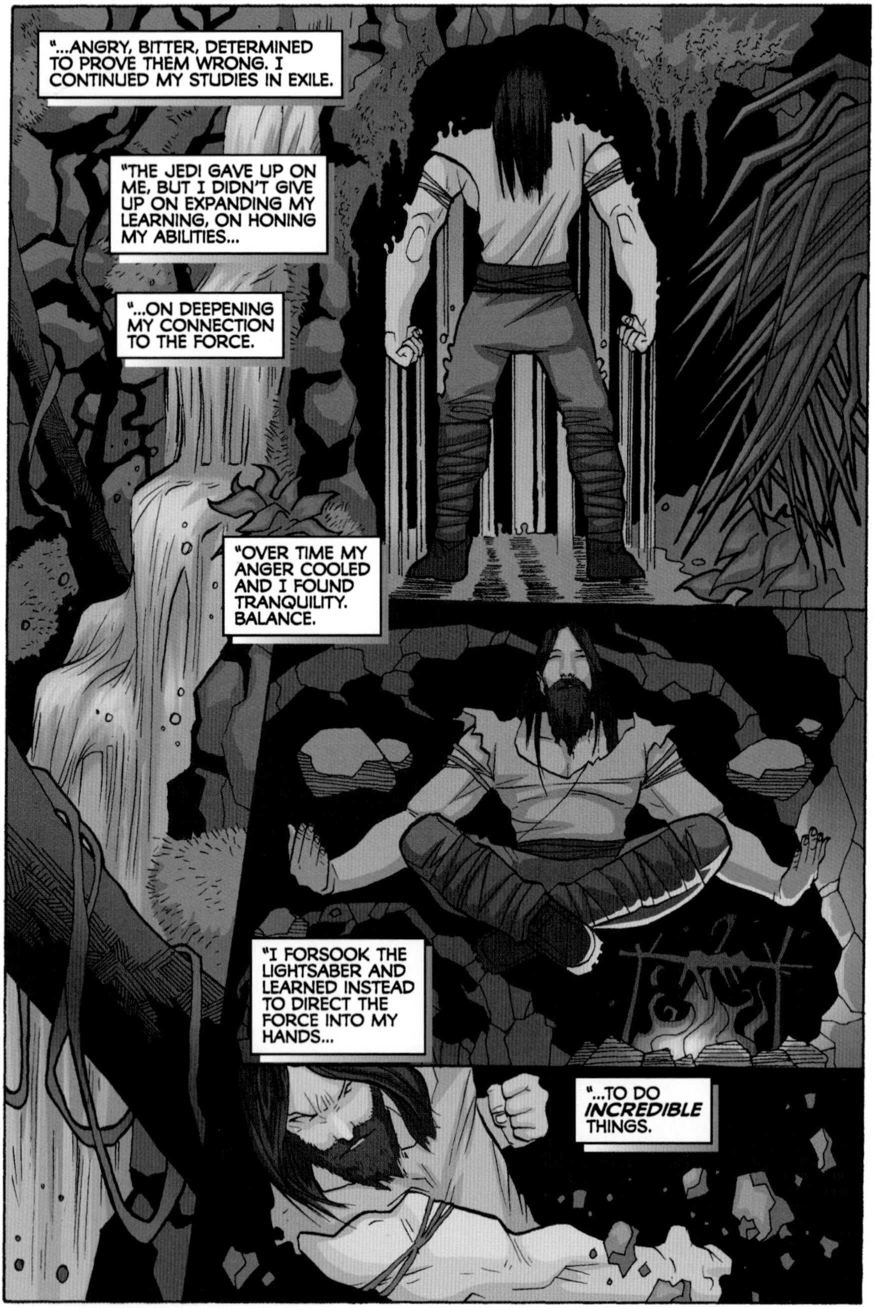
"...ANGRY, BITTER, DETERMINED TO PROVE THEM WRONG. I CONTINUED MY STUDIES IN EXILE.
"THE JEDI GAVE UP ON ME, BUT I DIDN'T GIVE UP ON EXPANDING MY LEARNING, ON HONING MY ABILITIES...
"...ON DEEPENING MY CONNECTION TO THE FORCE.
"OVER TIME MY ANGER COOLED AND I FOUND TRANQUILITY. BALANCE.
"I FORSOOK THE LIGHTSABER AND LEARNED INSTEAD TO DIRECT THE FORCE INTO MY HANDS...
"...TO DO *INCREDIBLE* THINGS.

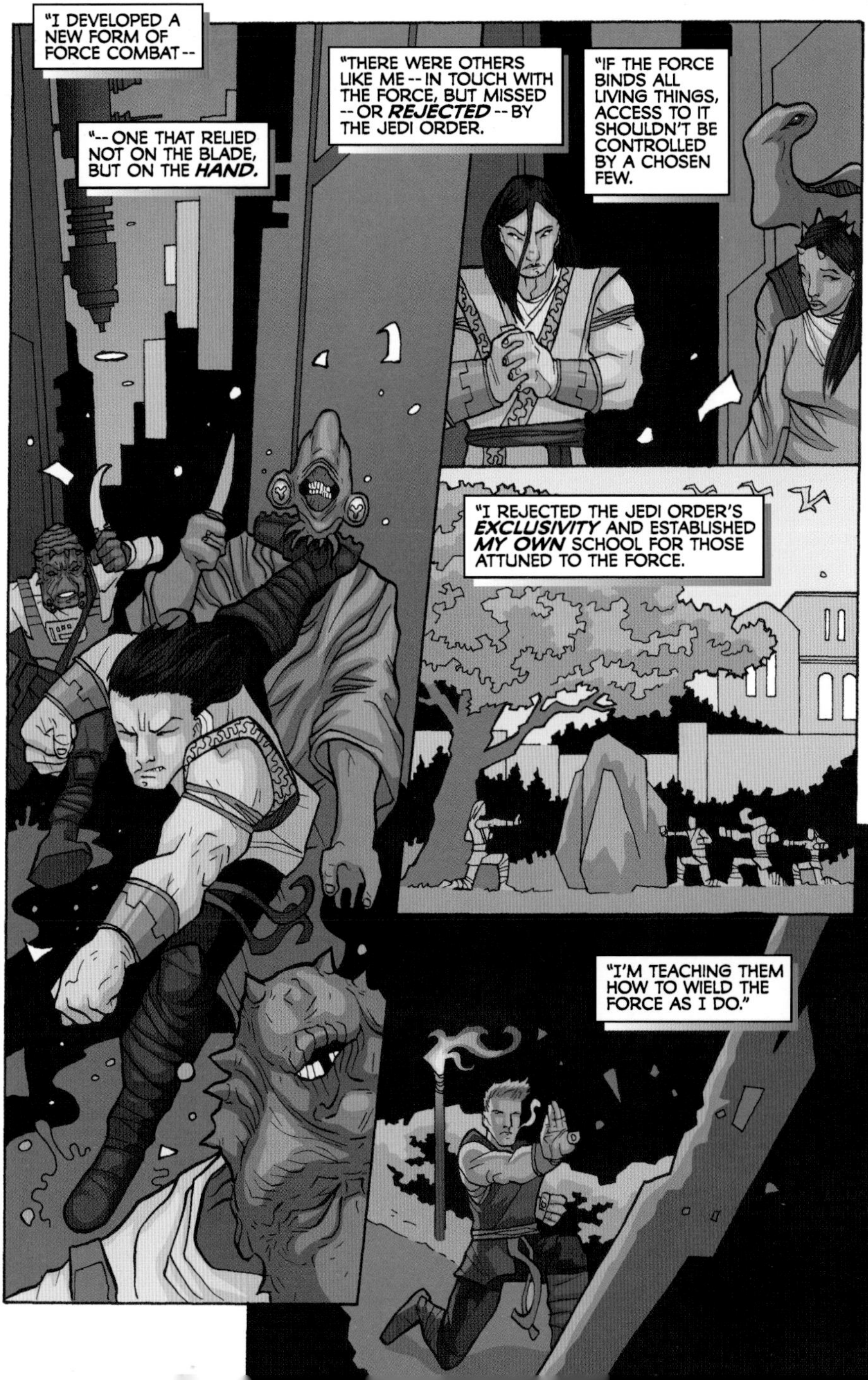
"I DEVELOPED A NEW FORM OF FORCE COMBAT--
"--ONE THAT RELIED NOT ON THE BLADE, BUT ON THE ***HAND.***
"THERE WERE OTHERS LIKE ME -- IN TOUCH WITH THE FORCE, BUT MISSED -- OR ***REJECTED*** -- BY THE JEDI ORDER.
"IF THE FORCE BINDS ALL LIVING THINGS, ACCESS TO IT SHOULDN'T BE CONTROLLED BY A CHOSEN FEW.
"I REJECTED THE JEDI ORDER'S ***EXCLUSIVITY*** AND ESTABLISHED ***MY OWN*** SCHOOL FOR THOSE ATTUNED TO THE FORCE.
"I'M TEACHING THEM HOW TO WIELD THE FORCE AS I DO."

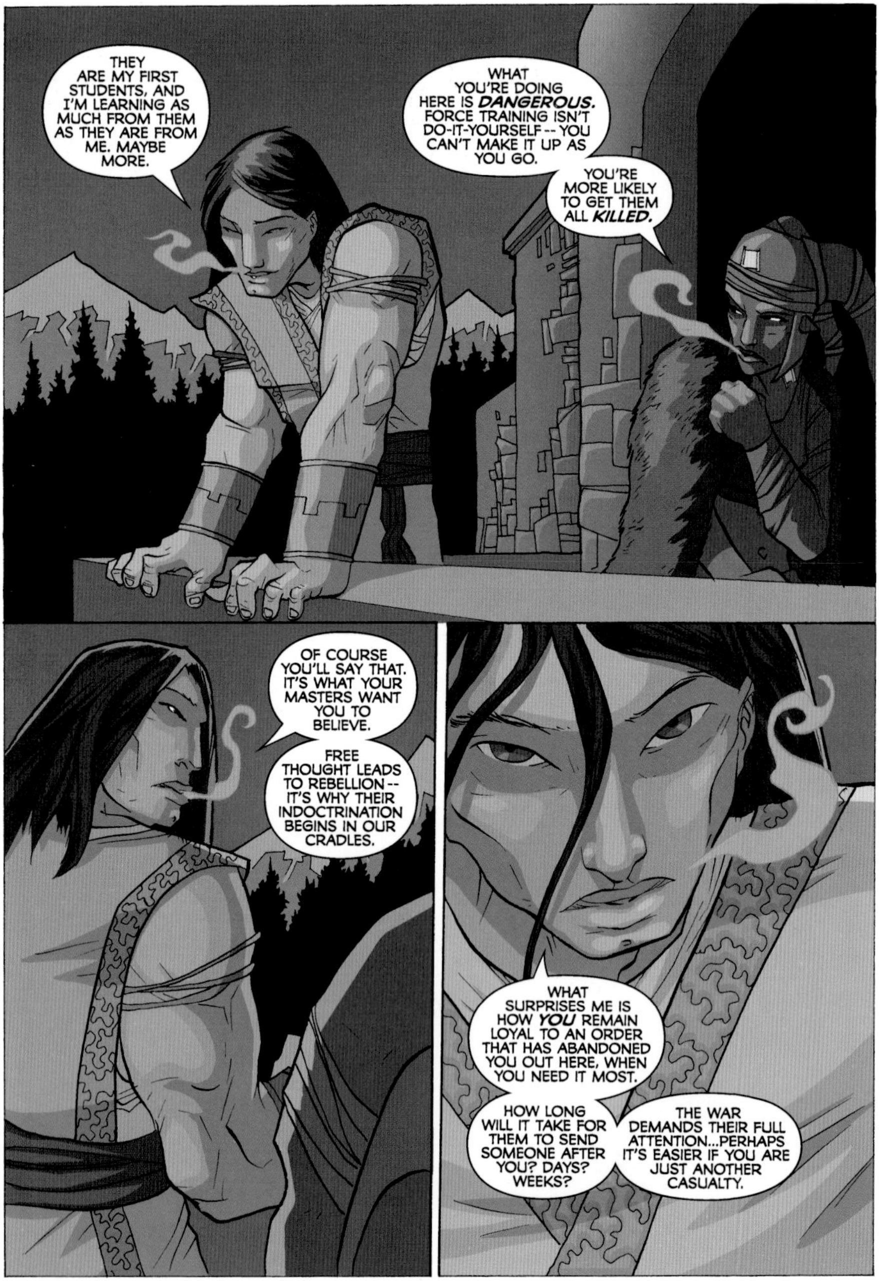
THEY ARE MY FIRST STUDENTS, AND I'M LEARNING AS MUCH FROM THEM AS THEY ARE FROM ME. MAYBE MORE.
WHAT YOU'RE DOING HERE IS DANGEROUS. FORCE TRAINING ISN'T DO-IT-YOURSELF -- YOU CAN'T MAKE IT UP AS YOU GO.
YOU'RE MORE LIKELY TO GET THEM ALL KILLED.
OF COURSE YOU'LL SAY THAT. IT'S WHAT YOUR MASTERS WANT YOU TO BELIEVE.
FREE THOUGHT LEADS TO REBELLION -- IT'S WHY THEIR INDOCTRINATION BEGINS IN OUR CRADLES.
WHAT SURPRISES ME IS HOW YOU REMAIN LOYAL TO AN ORDER THAT HAS ABANDONED YOU OUT HERE, WHEN YOU NEED IT MOST.
HOW LONG WILL IT TAKE FOR THEM TO SEND SOMEONE AFTER YOU? DAYS? WEEKS?
THE WAR DEMANDS THEIR FULL ATTENTION...PERHAPS IT'S EASIER IF YOU ARE JUST ANOTHER CASUALTY.

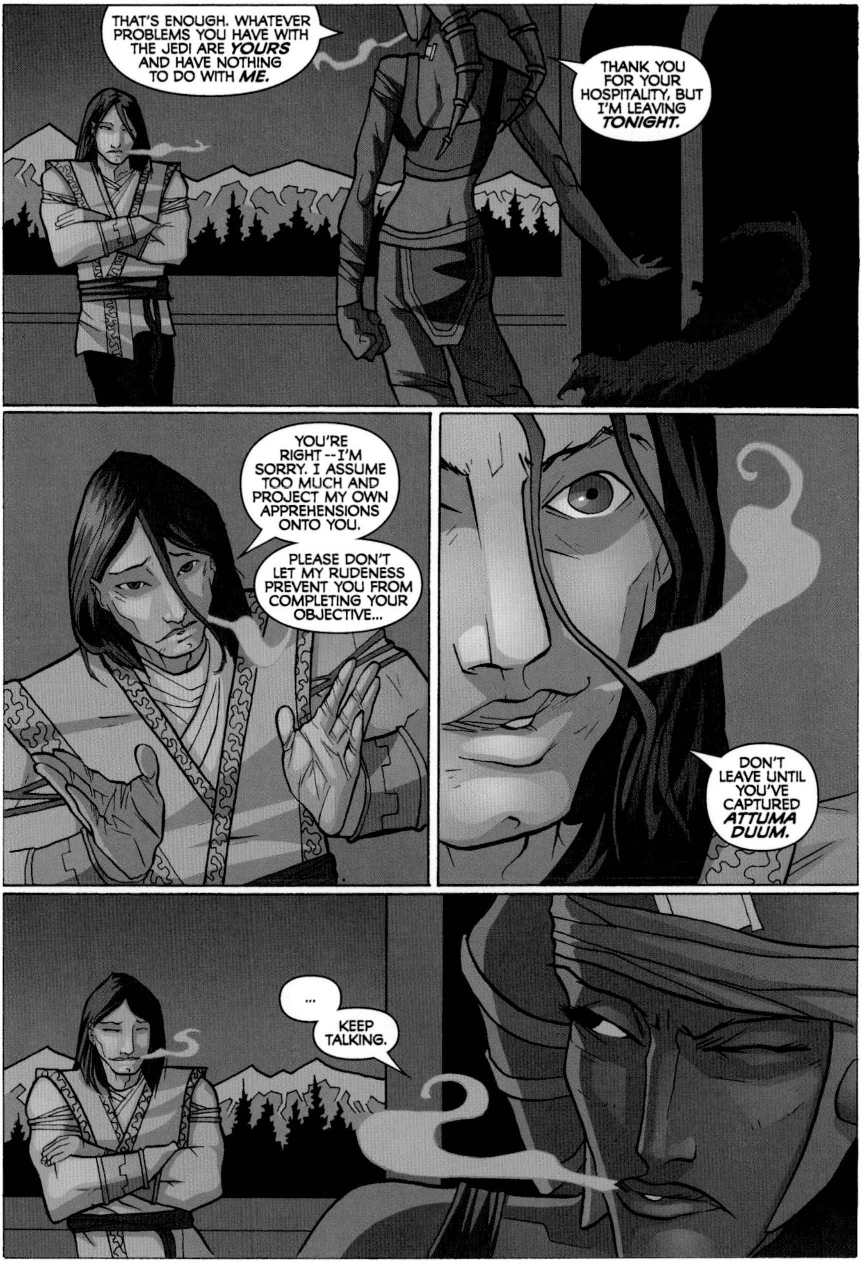
THAT'S ENOUGH. WHATEVER PROBLEMS YOU HAVE WITH THE JEDI ARE *YOURS* AND HAVE NOTHING TO DO WITH *ME.*
THANK YOU FOR YOUR HOSPITALITY, BUT I'M LEAVING *TONIGHT.*
YOU'RE RIGHT --I'M SORRY. I ASSUME TOO MUCH AND PROJECT MY OWN APPREHENSIONS ONTO YOU.
PLEASE DON'T LET MY RUDENESS PREVENT YOU FROM COMPLETING YOUR OBJECTIVE...
DON'T LEAVE UNTIL YOU'VE CAPTURED *ATTUMA DUUM.*
... KEEP TALKING.

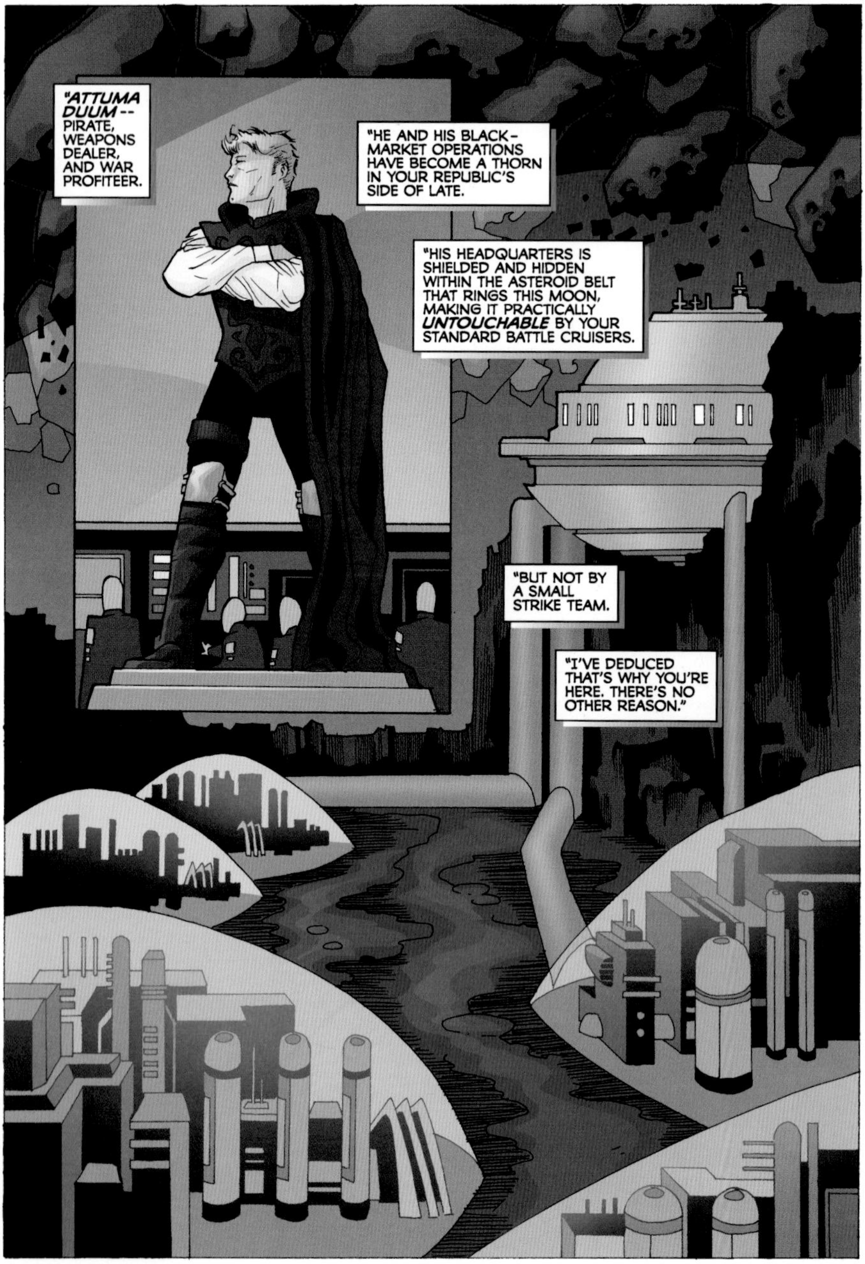
"ATTUMA DUUM -- PIRATE, WEAPONS DEALER, AND WAR PROFITEER.
"HE AND HIS BLACK-MARKET OPERATIONS HAVE BECOME A THORN IN YOUR REPUBLIC'S SIDE OF LATE.
"HIS HEADQUARTERS IS SHIELDED AND HIDDEN WITHIN THE ASTEROID BELT THAT RINGS THIS MOON, MAKING IT PRACTICALLY UNTOUCHABLE BY YOUR STANDARD BATTLE CRUISERS.
"BUT NOT BY A SMALL STRIKE TEAM.
"I'VE DEDUCED THAT'S WHY YOU'RE HERE. THERE'S NO OTHER REASON."

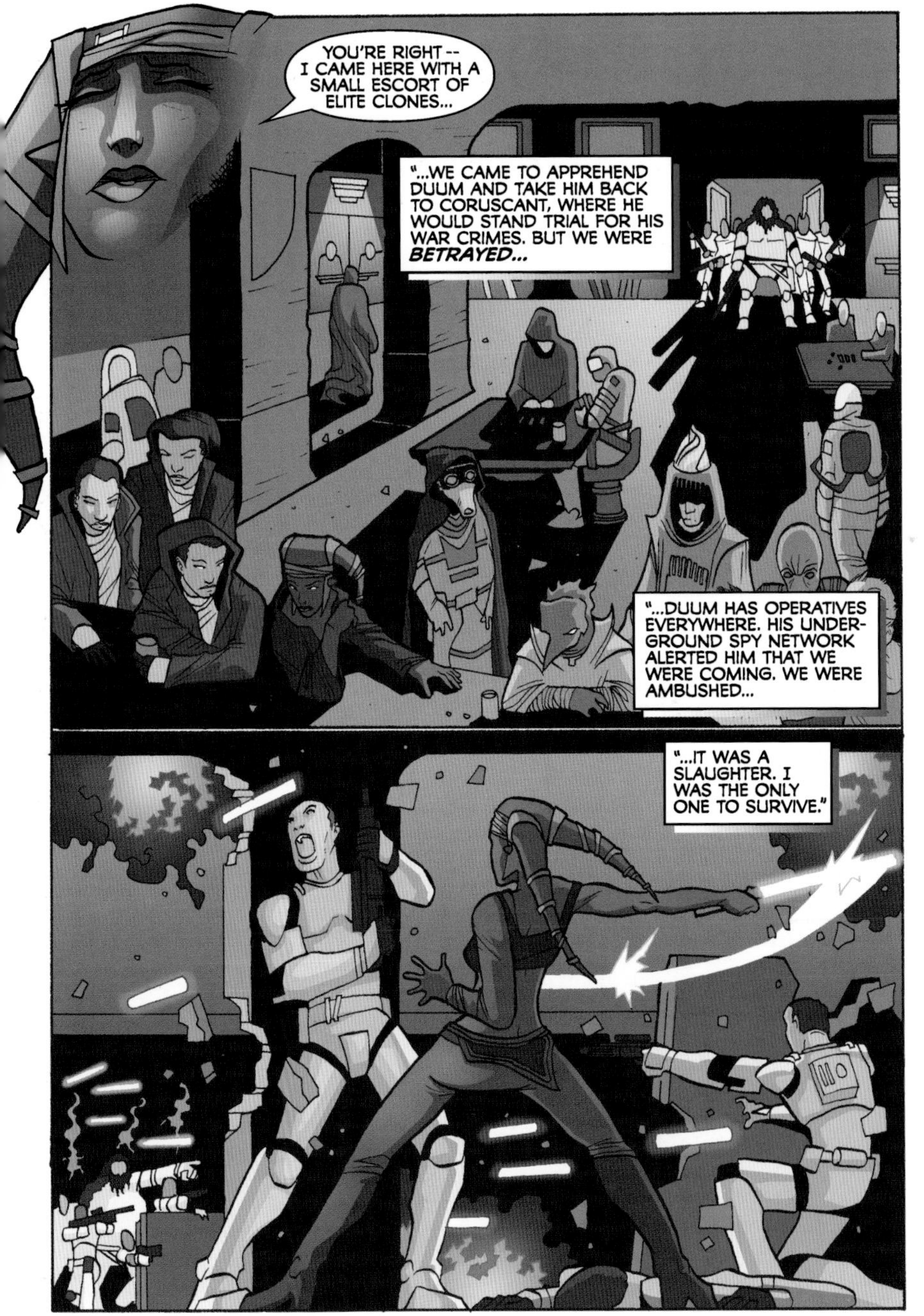
YOU'RE RIGHT -- I CAME HERE WITH A SMALL ESCORT OF ELITE CLONES...
"...WE CAME TO APPREHEND DUUM AND TAKE HIM BACK TO CORUSCANT, WHERE HE WOULD STAND TRIAL FOR HIS WAR CRIMES. BUT WE WERE *BETRAYED...*
"...DUUM HAS OPERATIVES EVERYWHERE. HIS UNDER-GROUND SPY NETWORK ALERTED HIM THAT WE WERE COMING. WE WERE AMBUSHED...
"...IT WAS A SLAUGHTER. I WAS THE ONLY ONE TO SURVIVE."

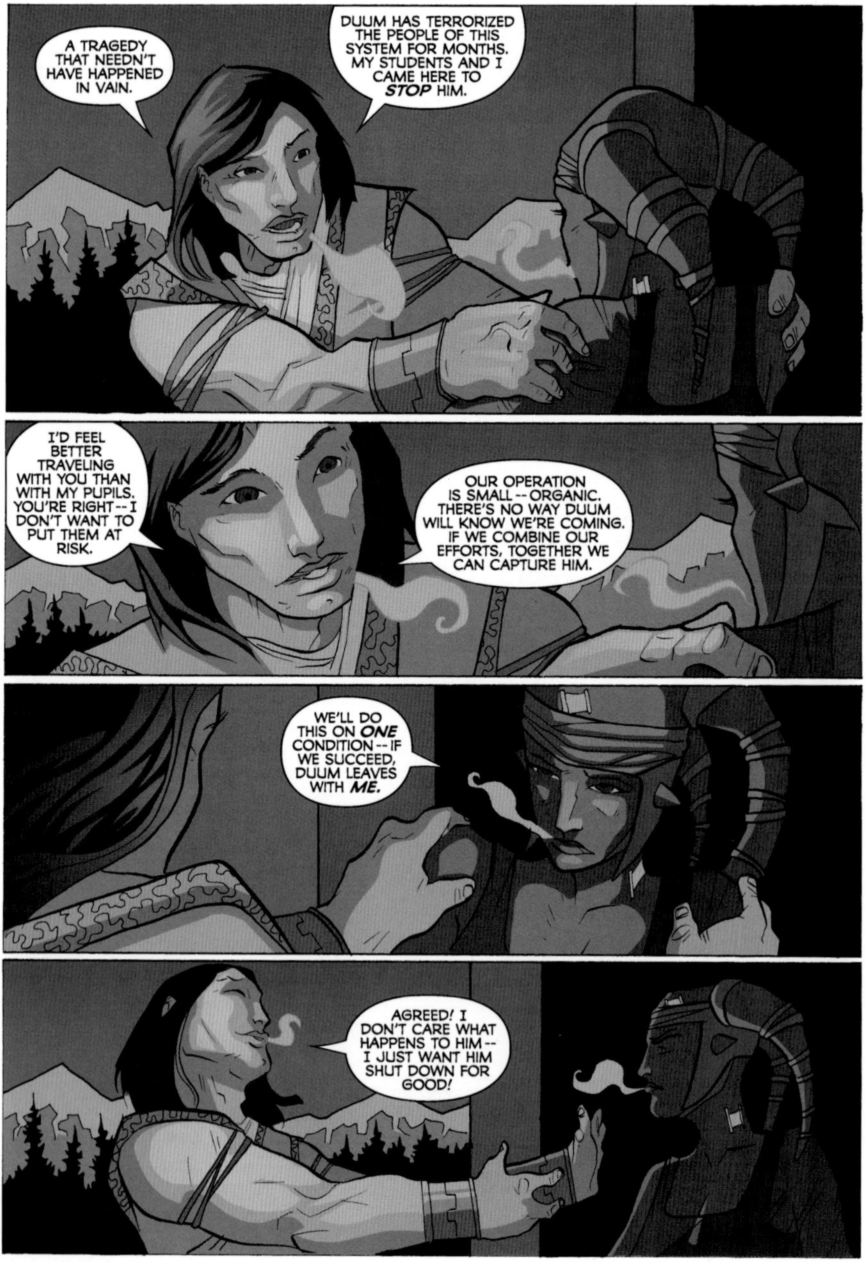
A TRAGEDY THAT NEEDN'T HAVE HAPPENED IN VAIN.
DUUM HAS TERRORIZED THE PEOPLE OF THIS SYSTEM FOR MONTHS. MY STUDENTS AND I CAME HERE TO ***STOP*** HIM.
I'D FEEL BETTER TRAVELING WITH YOU THAN WITH MY PUPILS. YOU'RE RIGHT--I DON'T WANT TO PUT THEM AT RISK.
OUR OPERATION IS SMALL--ORGANIC. THERE'S NO WAY DUUM WILL KNOW WE'RE COMING. IF WE COMBINE OUR EFFORTS, TOGETHER WE CAN CAPTURE HIM.
WE'LL DO THIS ON ***ONE*** CONDITION--IF WE SUCCEED, DUUM LEAVES WITH ***ME.***
AGREED! I DON'T CARE WHAT HAPPENS TO HIM--I JUST WANT HIM SHUT DOWN FOR GOOD!

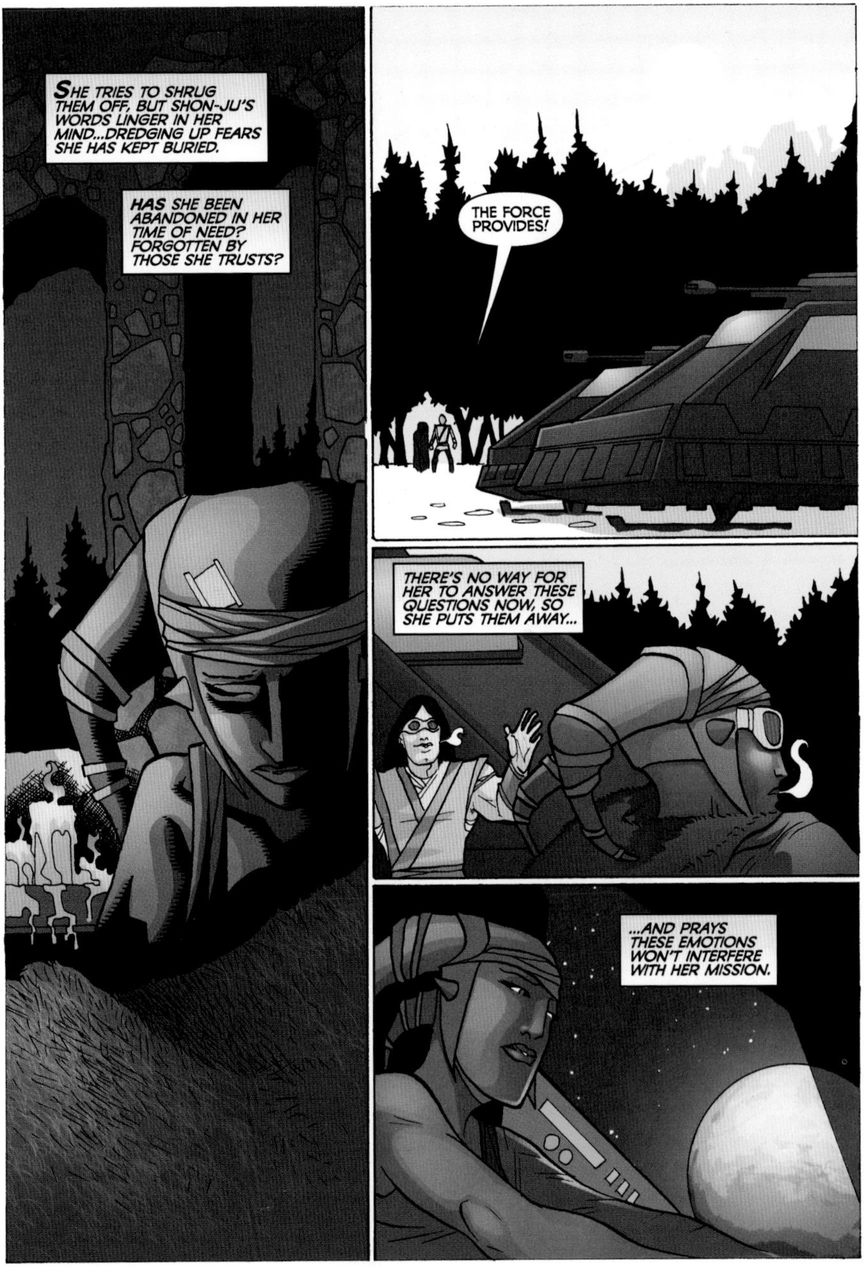
SHE TRIES TO SHRUG THEM OFF, BUT SHON-JU'S WORDS LINGER IN HER MIND...DREDGING UP FEARS SHE HAS KEPT BURIED.
HAS SHE BEEN ABANDONED IN HER TIME OF NEED? FORGOTTEN BY THOSE SHE TRUSTS?
THE FORCE PROVIDES!
THERE'S NO WAY FOR HER TO ANSWER THESE QUESTIONS NOW, SO SHE PUTS THEM AWAY...
...AND PRAYS THESE EMOTIONS WON'T INTERFERE WITH HER MISSION.

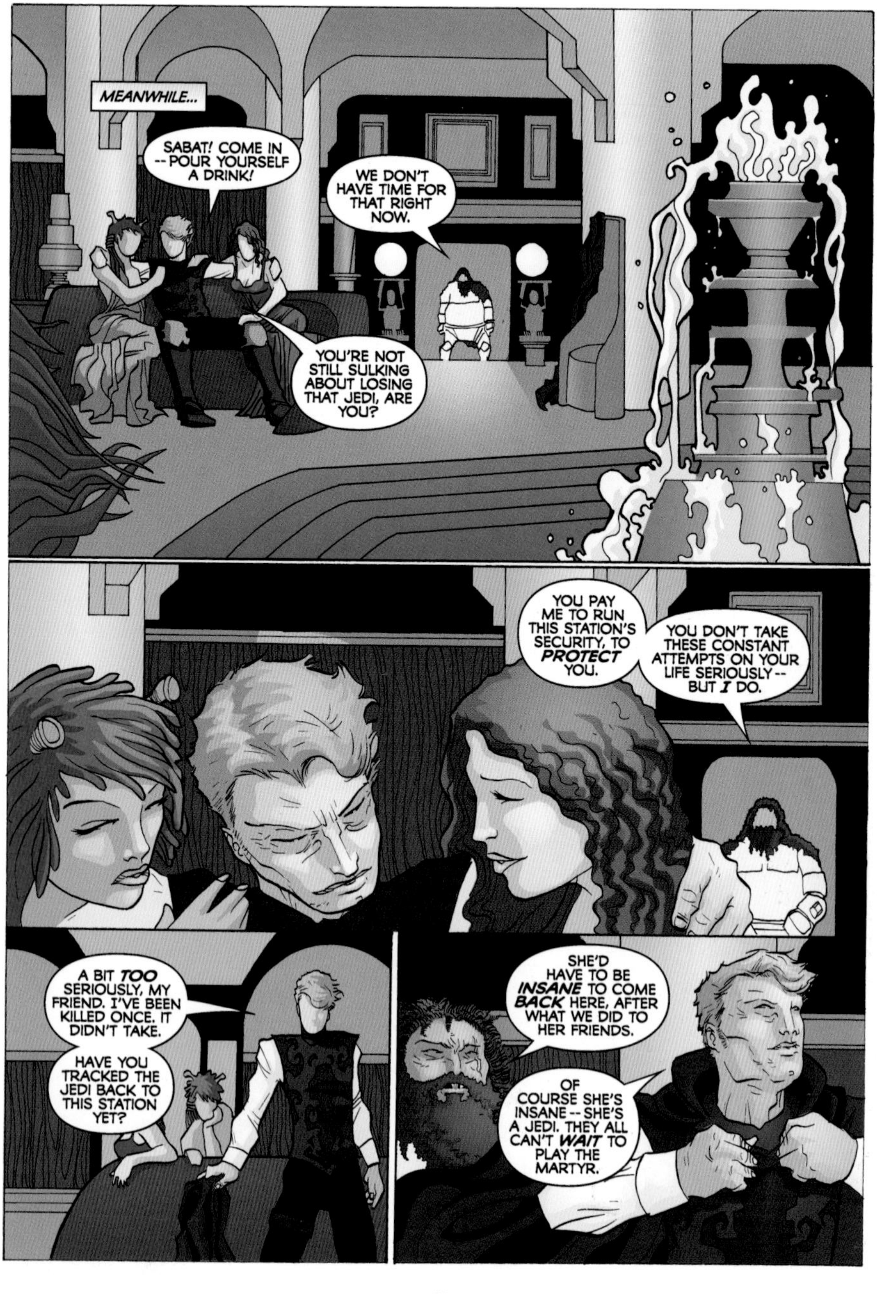
MEANWHILE...
SABAT! COME IN --POUR YOURSELF A DRINK!
WE DON'T HAVE TIME FOR THAT RIGHT NOW.
YOU'RE NOT STILL SULKING ABOUT LOSING THAT JEDI, ARE YOU?
YOU PAY ME TO RUN THIS STATION'S SECURITY, TO PROTECT YOU.
YOU DON'T TAKE THESE CONSTANT ATTEMPTS ON YOUR LIFE SERIOUSLY-- BUT I DO.
A BIT TOO SERIOUSLY, MY FRIEND. I'VE BEEN KILLED ONCE. IT DIDN'T TAKE.
HAVE YOU TRACKED THE JEDI BACK TO THIS STATION YET?
SHE'D HAVE TO BE INSANE TO COME BACK HERE, AFTER WHAT WE DID TO HER FRIENDS.
OF COURSE SHE'S INSANE -- SHE'S A JEDI. THEY ALL CAN'T WAIT TO PLAY THE MARTYR.

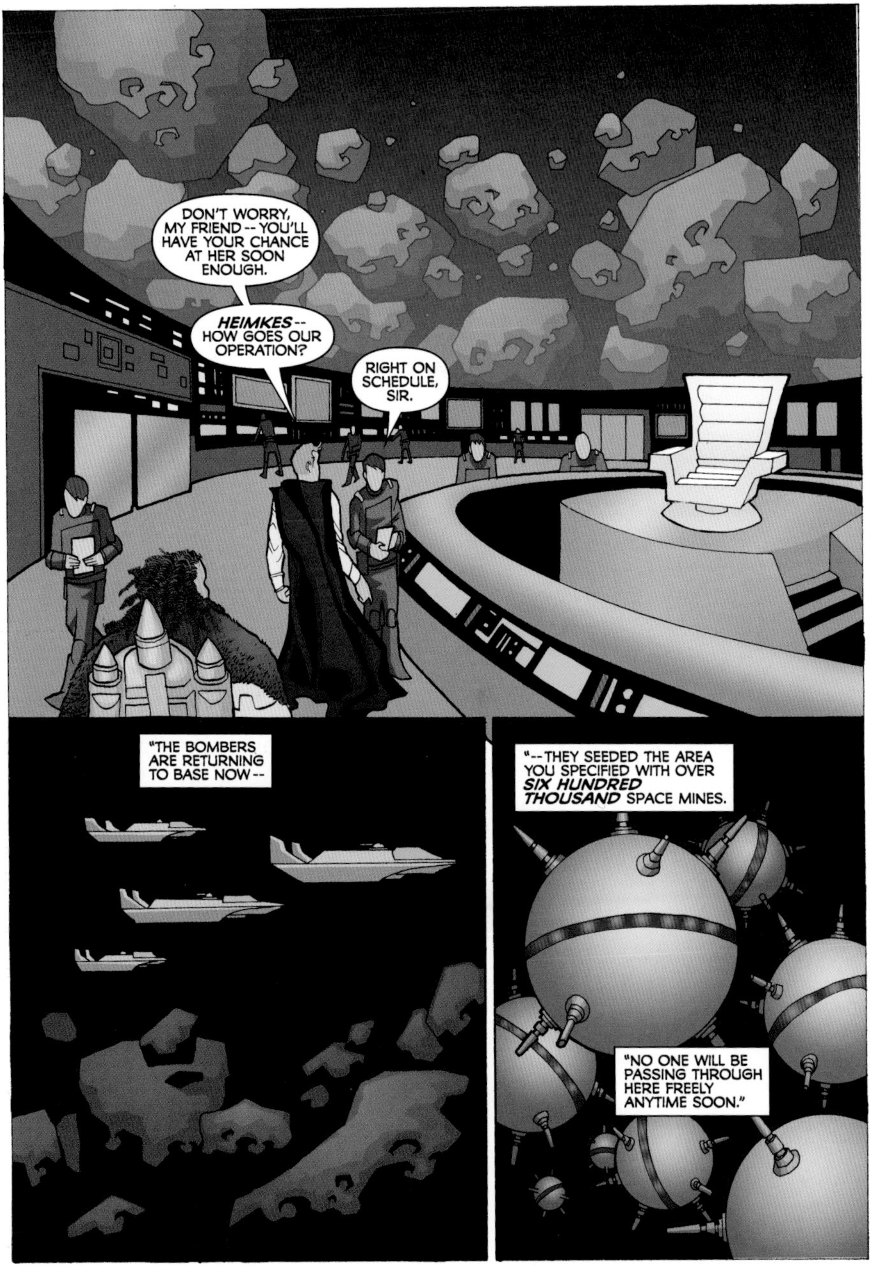
DON'T WORRY, MY FRIEND -- YOU'LL HAVE YOUR CHANCE AT HER SOON ENOUGH.
HEIMKES -- HOW GOES OUR OPERATION?
RIGHT ON SCHEDULE, SIR.
"THE BOMBERS ARE RETURNING TO BASE NOW --
"-- THEY SEEDED THE AREA YOU SPECIFIED WITH OVER *SIX HUNDRED THOUSAND* SPACE MINES.
"NO ONE WILL BE PASSING THROUGH HERE FREELY ANYTIME SOON."

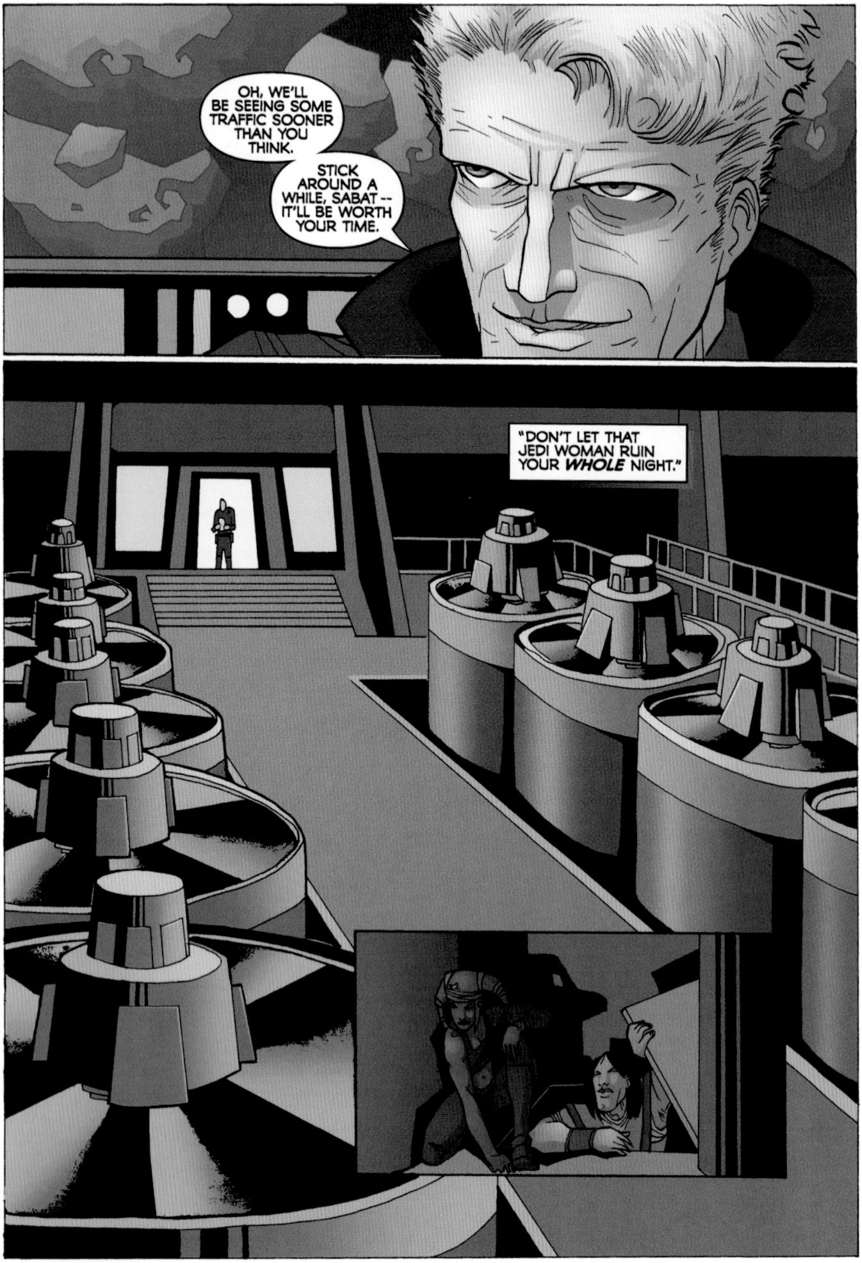
OH, WE'LL BE SEEING SOME TRAFFIC SOONER THAN YOU THINK.
STICK AROUND A WHILE, SABAT -- IT'LL BE WORTH YOUR TIME.
"DON'T LET THAT JEDI WOMAN RUIN YOUR *WHOLE* NIGHT."

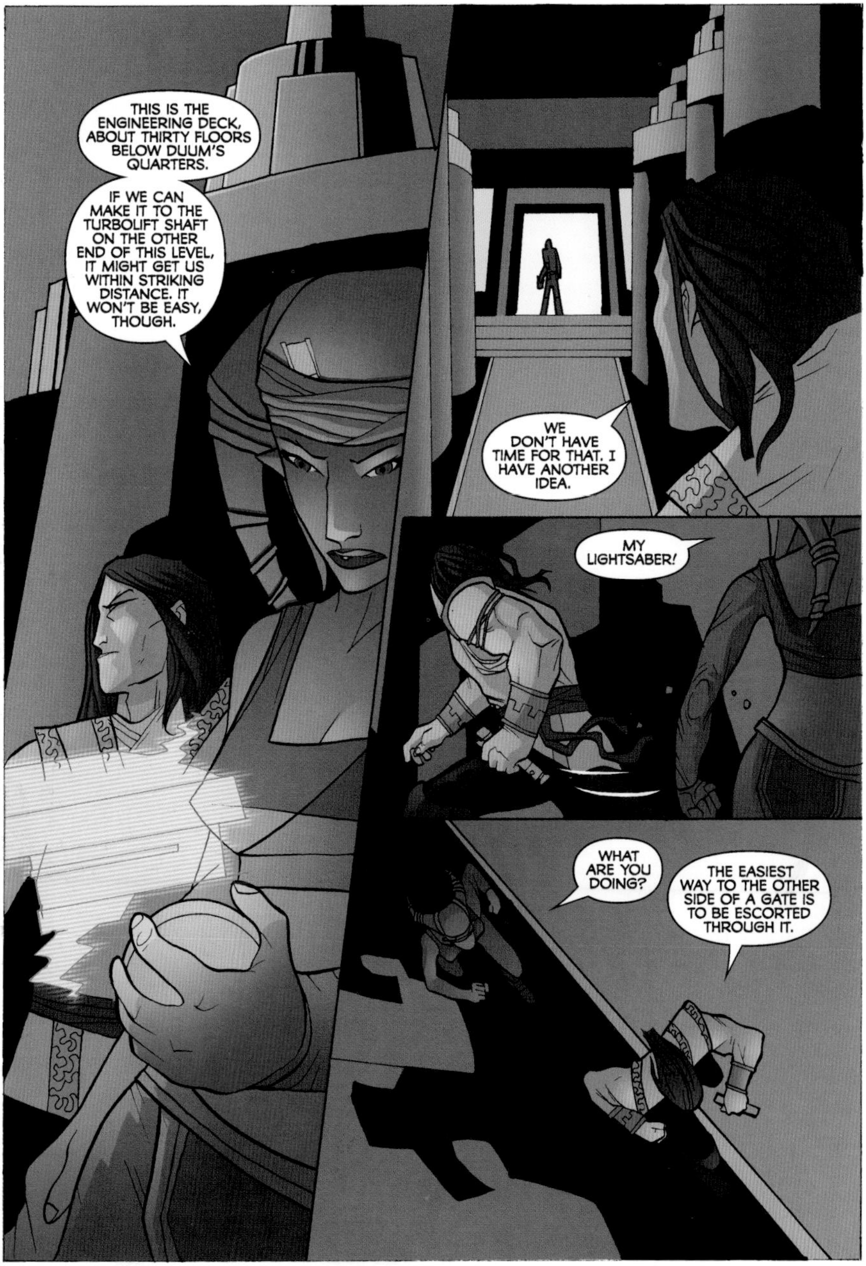
THIS IS THE ENGINEERING DECK, ABOUT THIRTY FLOORS BELOW DUUM'S QUARTERS.
IF WE CAN MAKE IT TO THE TURBOLIFT SHAFT ON THE OTHER END OF THIS LEVEL, IT MIGHT GET US WITHIN STRIKING DISTANCE. IT WON'T BE EASY, THOUGH.
WE DON'T HAVE TIME FOR THAT. I HAVE ANOTHER IDEA.
MY LIGHTSABER!
WHAT ARE YOU DOING?
THE EASIEST WAY TO THE OTHER SIDE OF A GATE IS TO BE ESCORTED THROUGH IT.

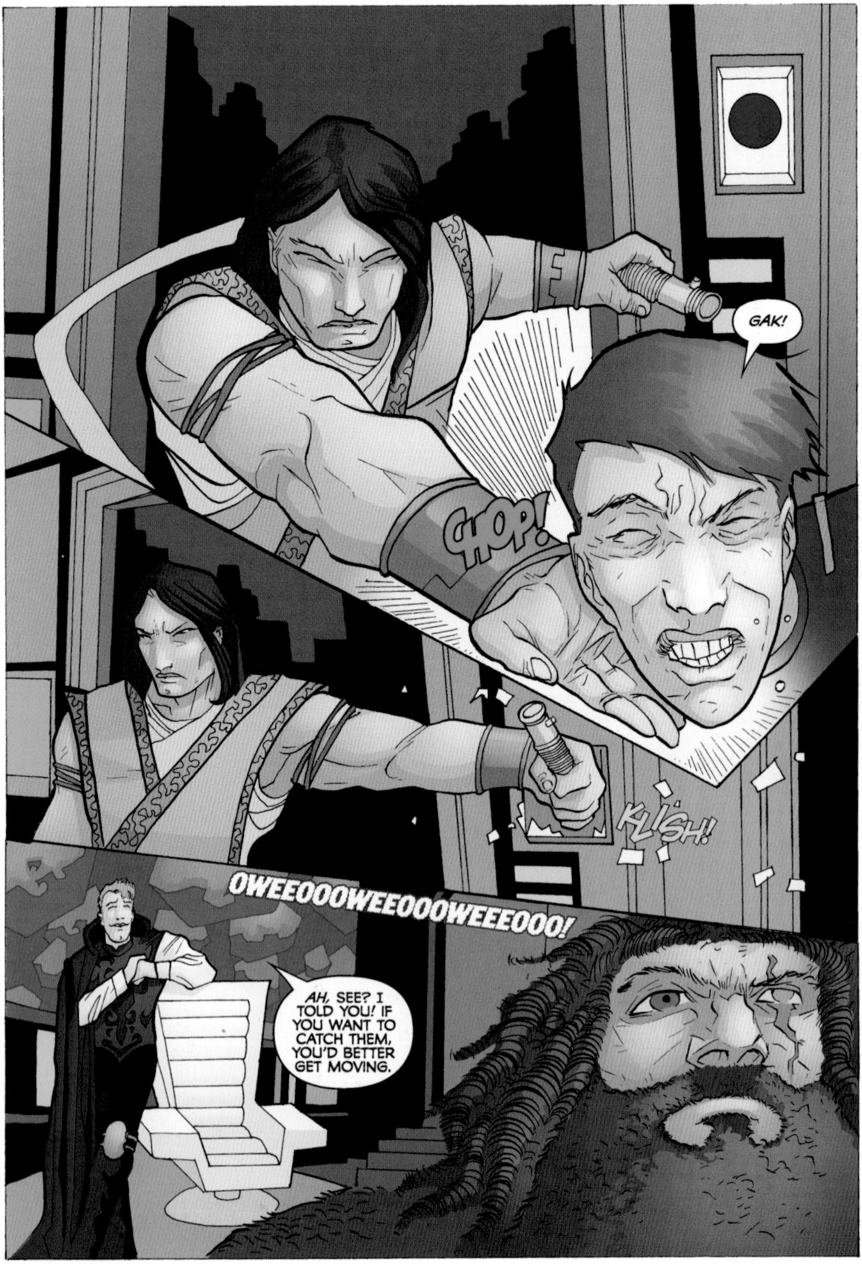
GAK!
CHOP!
KLISH!
OWEEOOOWEEOOOWEEEOOO!
AH, SEE? I TOLD YOU! IF YOU WANT TO CATCH THEM, YOU'D BETTER GET MOVING.

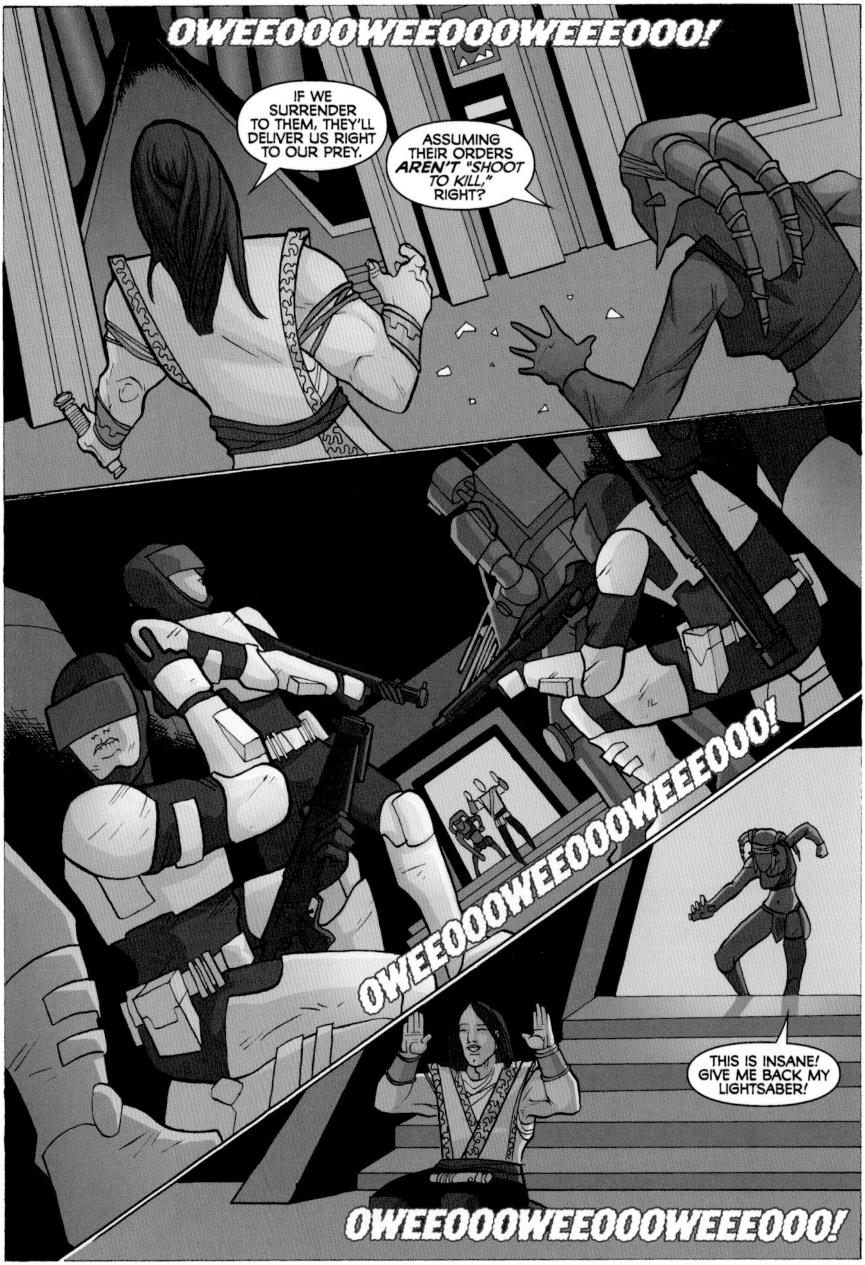
OWEEOOOWEEOOOWEEEOOO!
IF WE SURRENDER TO THEM, THEY'LL DELIVER US RIGHT TO OUR PREY.
ASSUMING THEIR ORDERS ***AREN'T*** *"SHOOT TO KILL,"* RIGHT?
OWEEOOOWEEOOOWEEEOOO!
THIS IS INSANE! GIVE ME BACK MY LIGHTSABER!
OWEEOOOWEEOOOWEEEOOO!

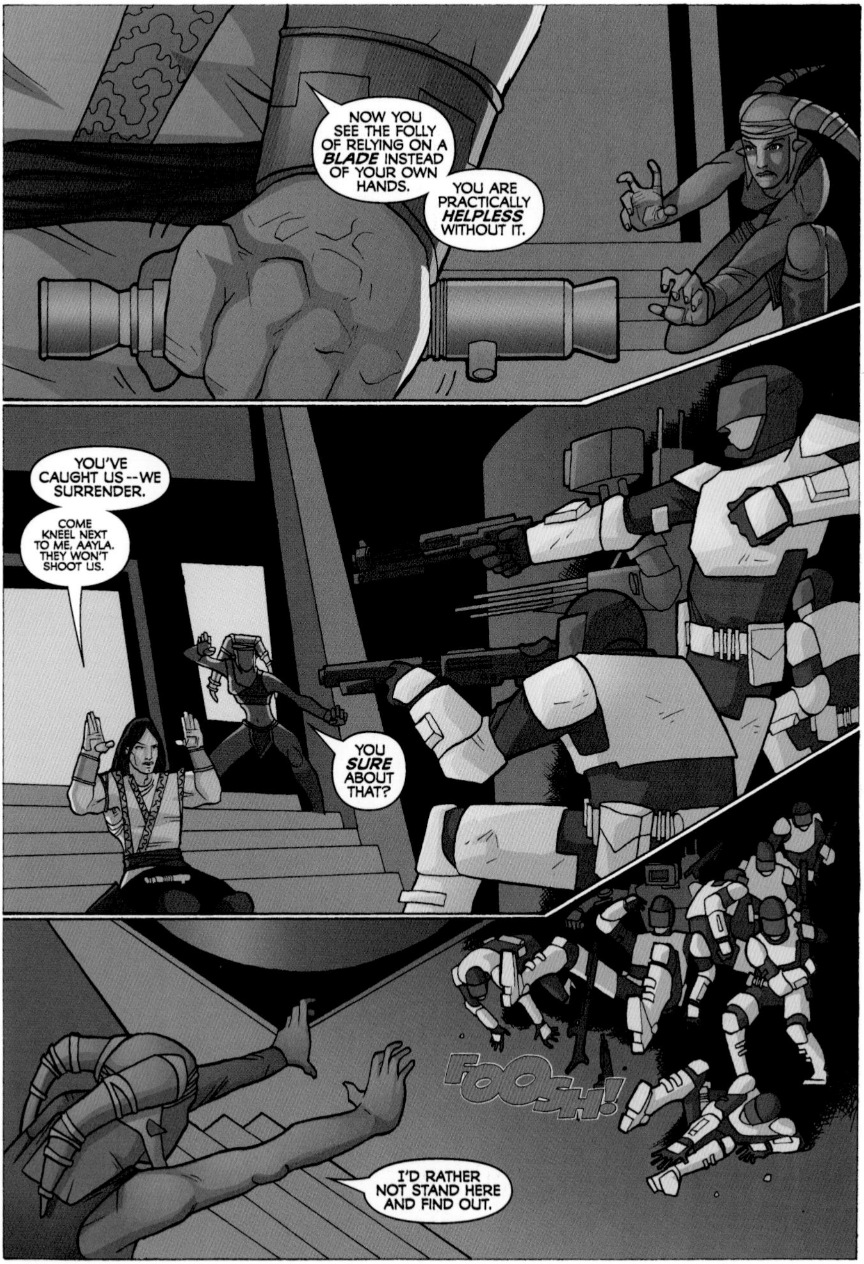
NOW YOU SEE THE FOLLY OF RELYING ON A *BLADE* INSTEAD OF YOUR OWN HANDS.
YOU ARE PRACTICALLY *HELPLESS* WITHOUT IT.
YOU'VE CAUGHT US--WE SURRENDER.
COME KNEEL NEXT TO ME, AAYLA. THEY WON'T SHOOT US.
YOU *SURE* ABOUT THAT?
FOOSH!
I'D RATHER NOT STAND HERE AND FIND OUT.

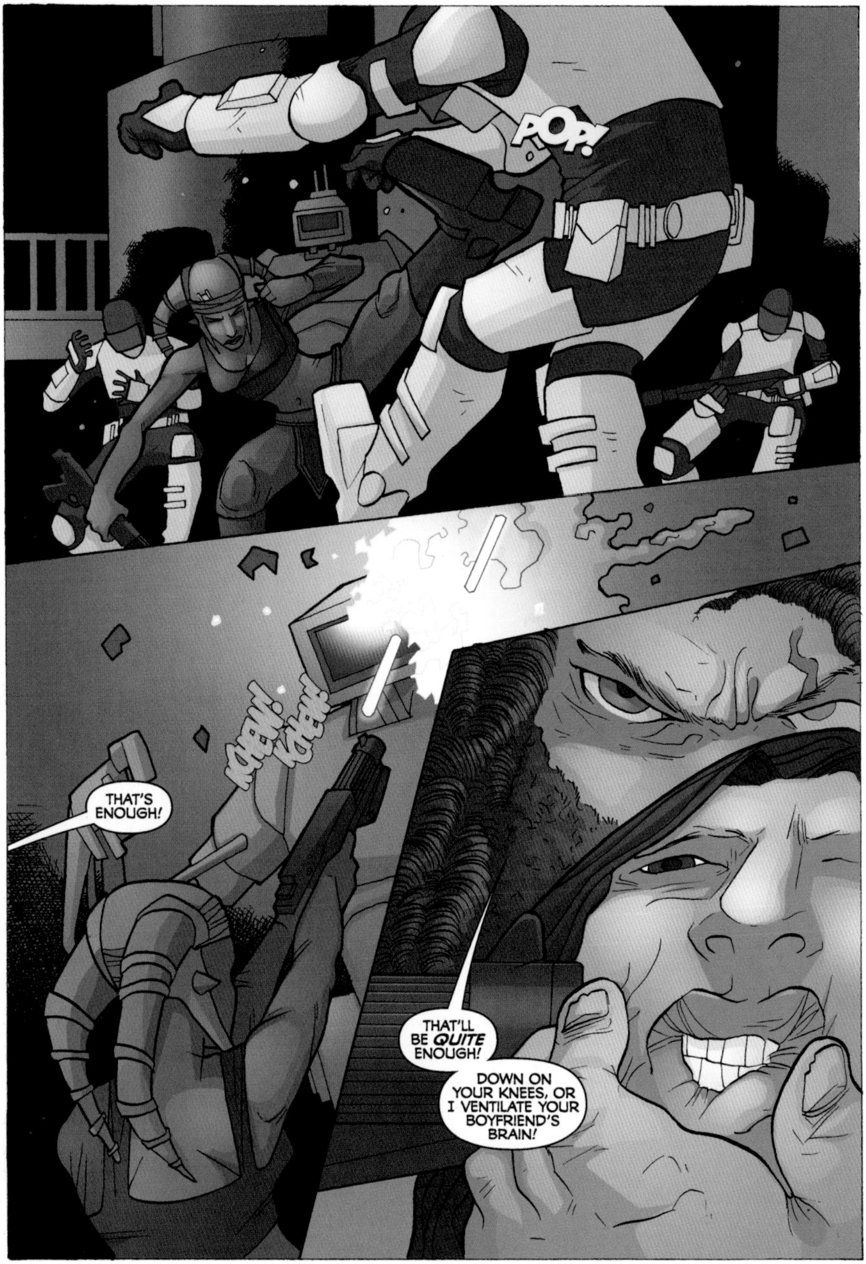
POP!
KCHEW! KCHEW!
THAT'S ENOUGH!
THAT'LL BE ***QUITE*** ENOUGH!
DOWN ON YOUR KNEES, OR I VENTILATE YOUR BOYFRIEND'S BRAIN!

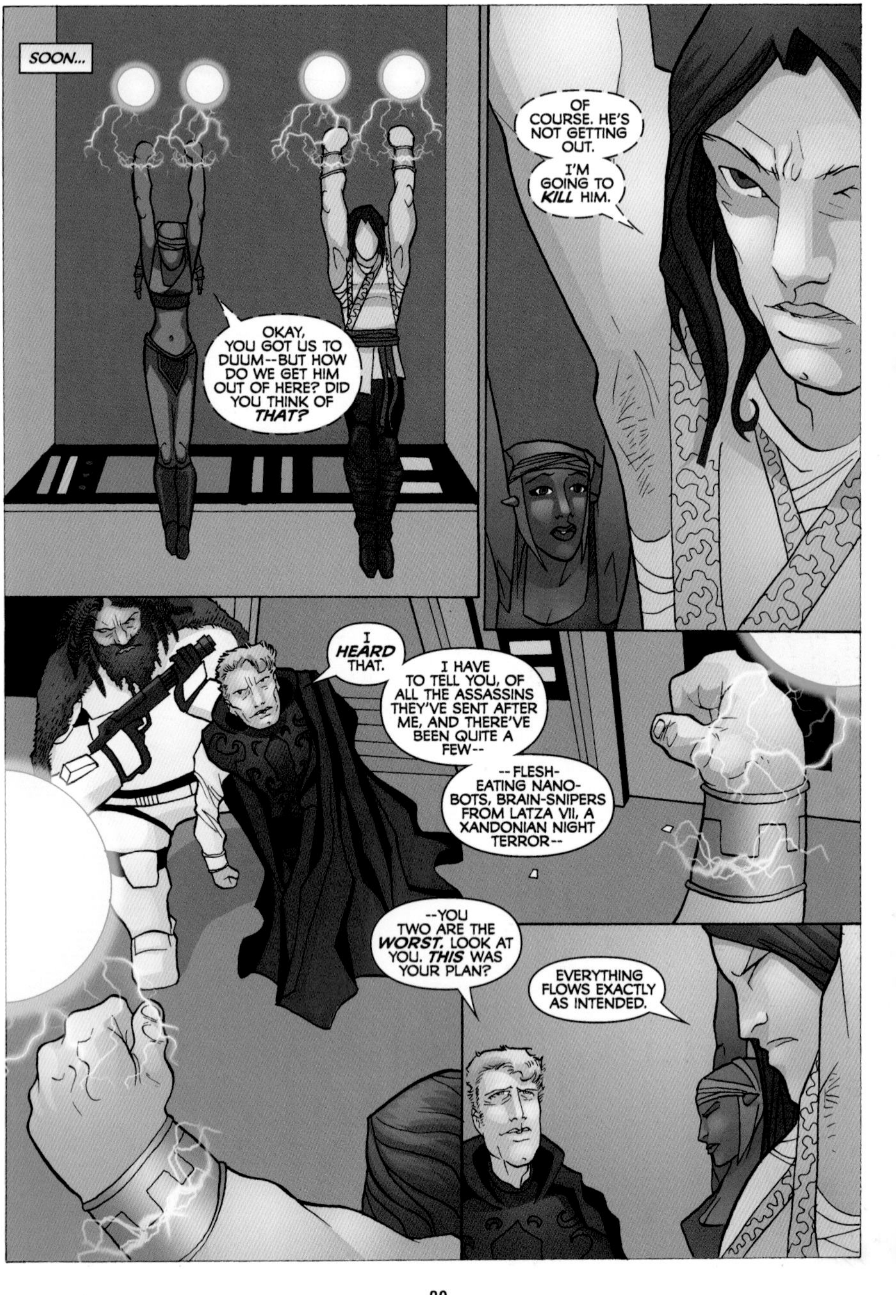
SOON...
OKAY, YOU GOT US TO DUUM--BUT HOW DO WE GET HIM OUT OF HERE? DID YOU THINK OF THAT?
OF COURSE. HE'S NOT GETTING OUT.
I'M GOING TO KILL HIM.
I HEARD THAT.
I HAVE TO TELL YOU, OF ALL THE ASSASSINS THEY'VE SENT AFTER ME, AND THERE'VE BEEN QUITE A FEW--
--FLESH-EATING NANO-BOTS, BRAIN-SNIPERS FROM LATZA VII, A XANDONIAN NIGHT TERROR--
--YOU TWO ARE THE WORST. LOOK AT YOU. THIS WAS YOUR PLAN?
EVERYTHING FLOWS EXACTLY AS INTENDED.

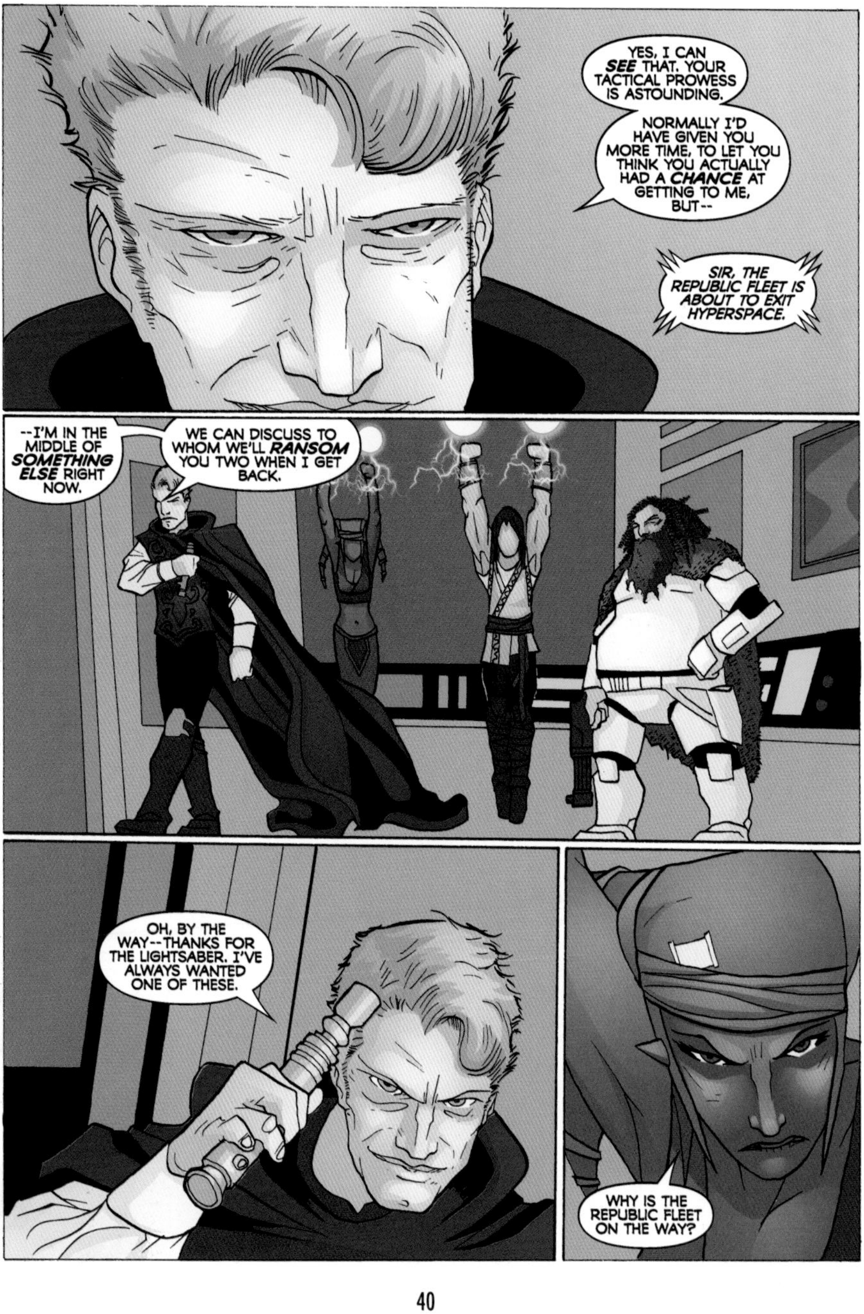
YES, I CAN SEE THAT. YOUR TACTICAL PROWESS IS ASTOUNDING.
NORMALLY I'D HAVE GIVEN YOU MORE TIME, TO LET YOU THINK YOU ACTUALLY HAD A CHANCE AT GETTING TO ME, BUT--
SIR, THE REPUBLIC FLEET IS ABOUT TO EXIT HYPERSPACE.
--I'M IN THE MIDDLE OF SOMETHING ELSE RIGHT NOW.
WE CAN DISCUSS TO WHOM WE'LL RANSOM YOU TWO WHEN I GET BACK.
OH, BY THE WAY--THANKS FOR THE LIGHTSABER. I'VE ALWAYS WANTED ONE OF THESE.
WHY IS THE REPUBLIC FLEET ON THE WAY?

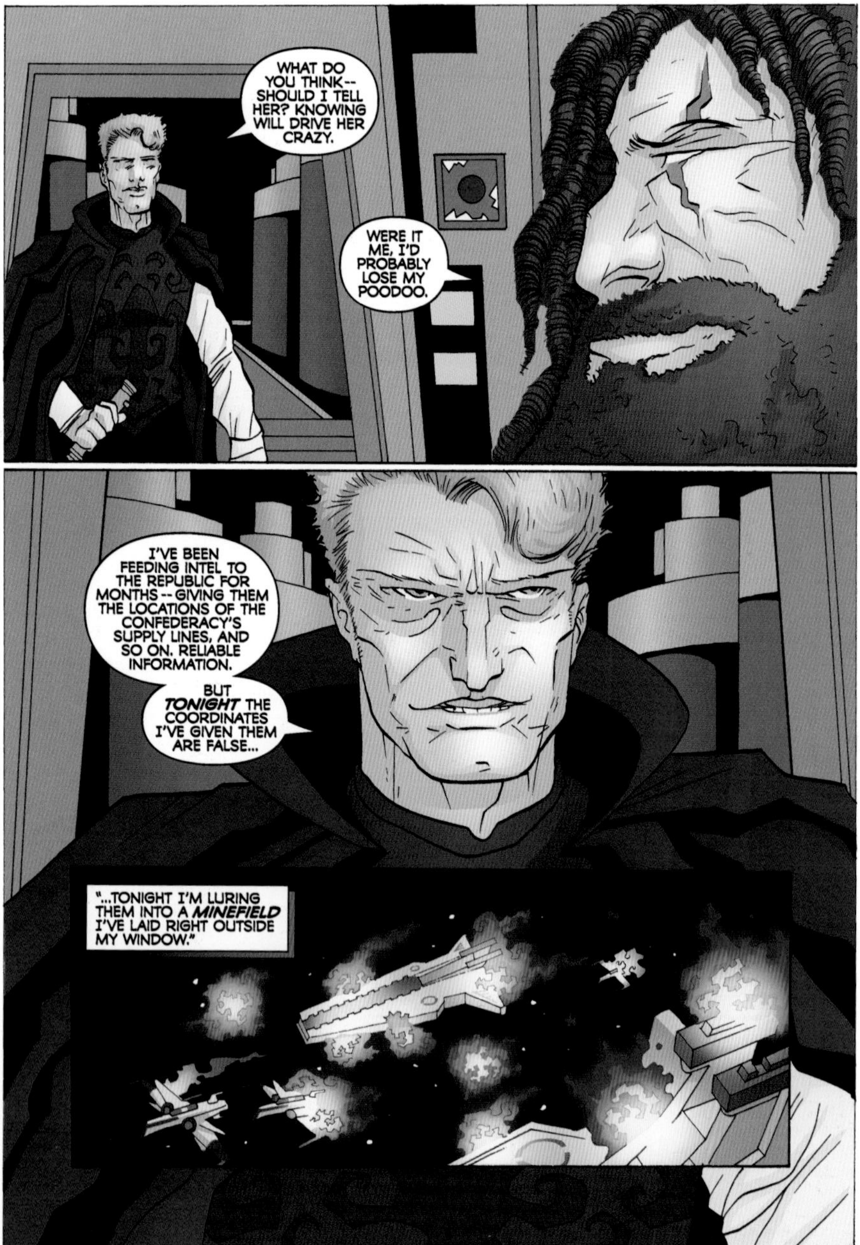
WHAT DO YOU THINK-- SHOULD I TELL HER? KNOWING WILL DRIVE HER CRAZY.
WERE IT ME, I'D PROBABLY LOSE MY POODOO.
I'VE BEEN FEEDING INTEL TO THE REPUBLIC FOR MONTHS -- GIVING THEM THE LOCATIONS OF THE CONFEDERACY'S SUPPLY LINES, AND SO ON. RELIABLE INFORMATION.
BUT *TONIGHT* THE COORDINATES I'VE GIVEN THEM ARE FALSE...
"...TONIGHT I'M LURING THEM INTO A *MINEFIELD* I'VE LAID RIGHT OUTSIDE MY WINDOW."

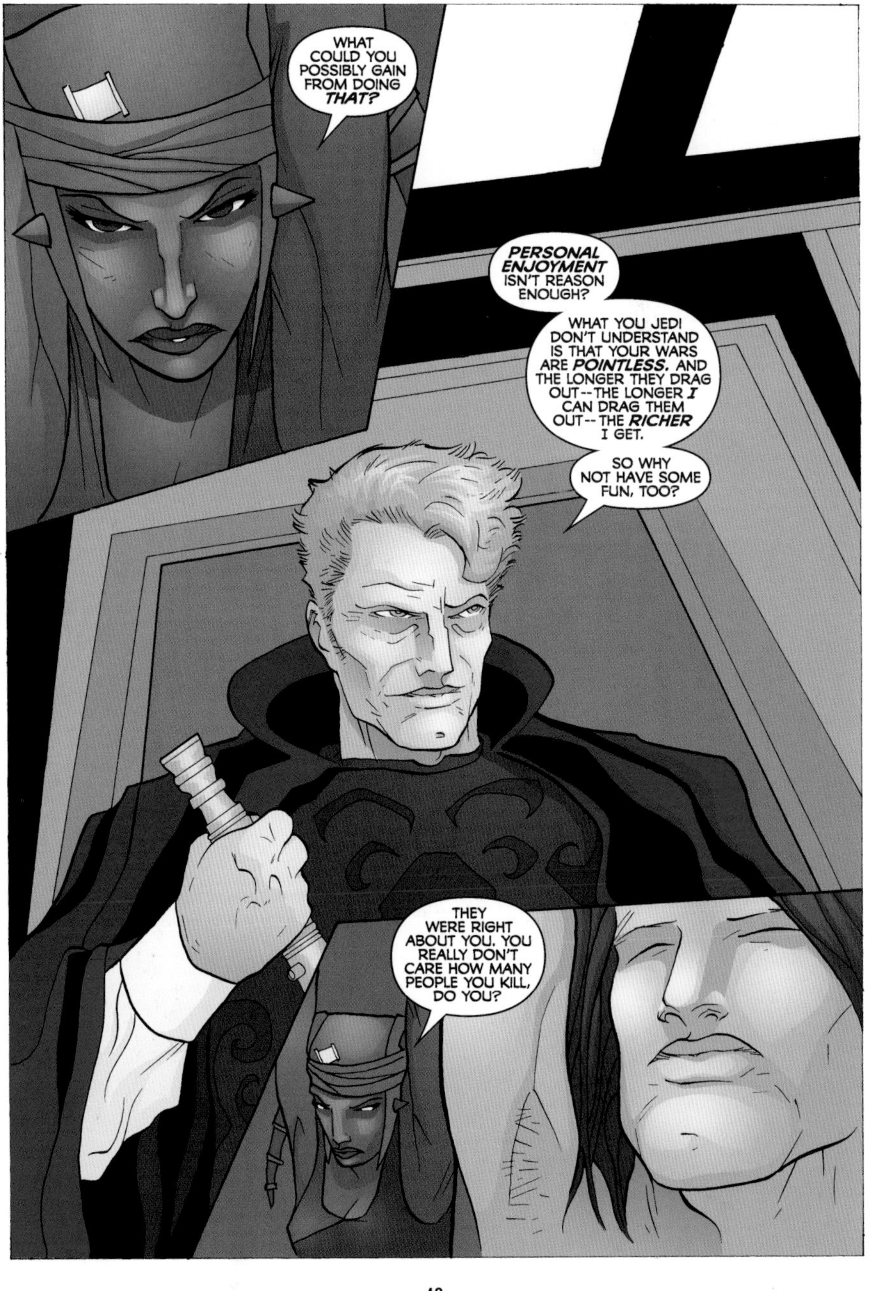
WHAT COULD YOU POSSIBLY GAIN FROM DOING *THAT?*
PERSONAL ENJOYMENT ISN'T REASON ENOUGH?
WHAT YOU JEDI DON'T UNDERSTAND IS THAT YOUR WARS ARE *POINTLESS.* AND THE LONGER THEY DRAG OUT--THE LONGER *I* CAN DRAG THEM OUT--THE *RICHER* I GET.
SO WHY NOT HAVE SOME FUN, TOO?
THEY WERE RIGHT ABOUT YOU. YOU REALLY DON'T CARE HOW MANY PEOPLE YOU KILL, DO YOU?

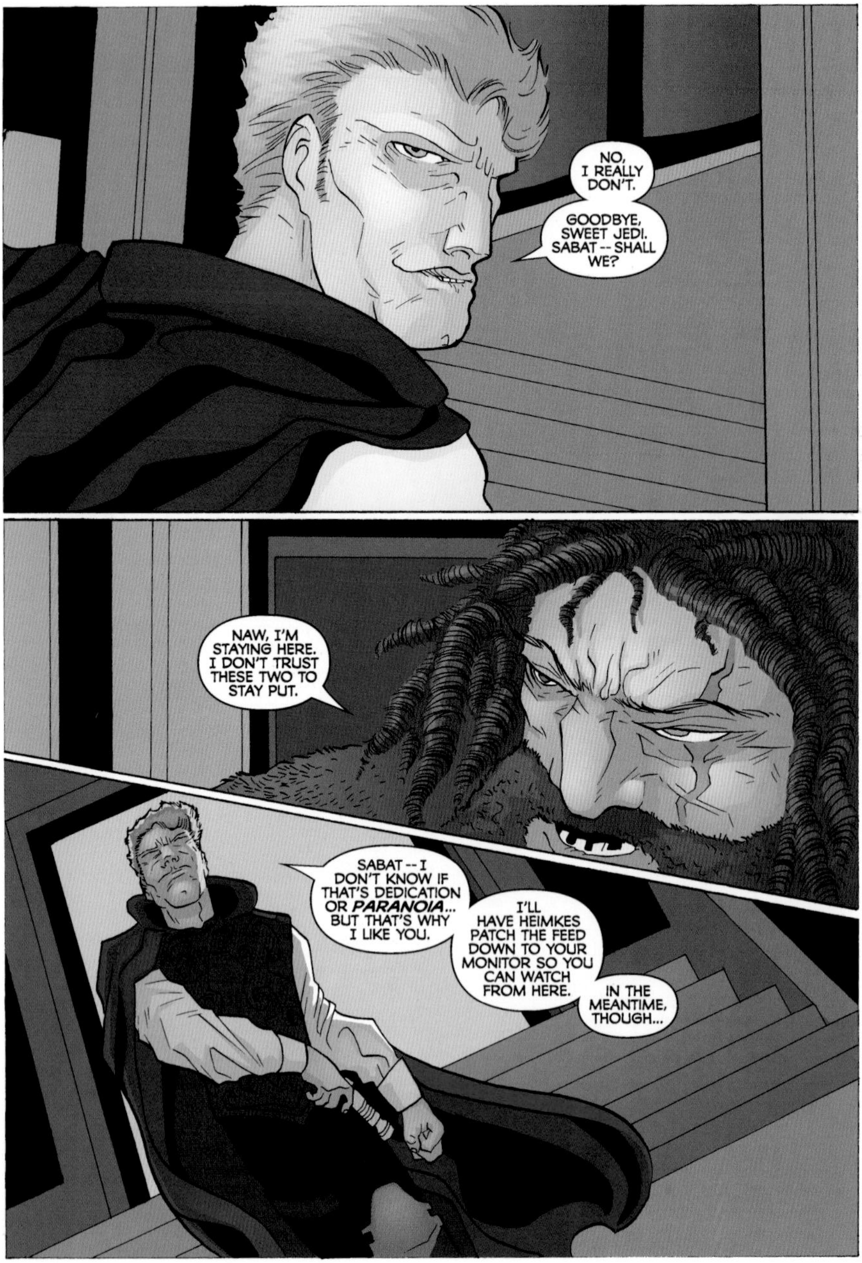
NO, I REALLY DON'T.
GOODBYE, SWEET JEDI. SABAT -- SHALL WE?
NAW, I'M STAYING HERE. I DON'T TRUST THESE TWO TO STAY PUT.
SABAT -- I DON'T KNOW IF THAT'S DEDICATION OR *PARANOIA*... BUT THAT'S WHY I LIKE YOU.
I'LL HAVE HEIMKES PATCH THE FEED DOWN TO YOUR MONITOR SO YOU CAN WATCH FROM HERE.
IN THE MEANTIME, THOUGH...

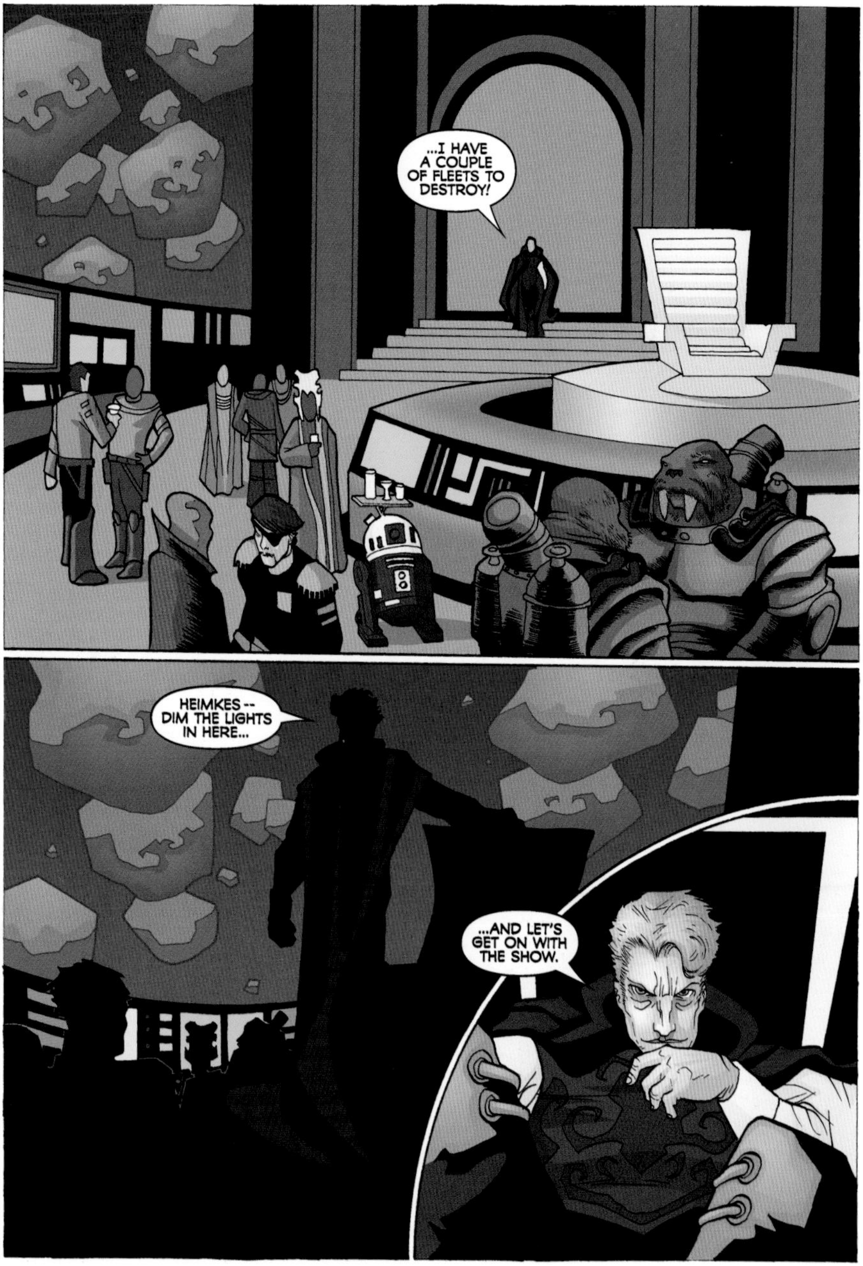

...I HAVE A COUPLE OF FLEETS TO DESTROY!
HEIMKES -- DIM THE LIGHTS IN HERE...
...AND LET'S GET ON WITH THE SHOW.

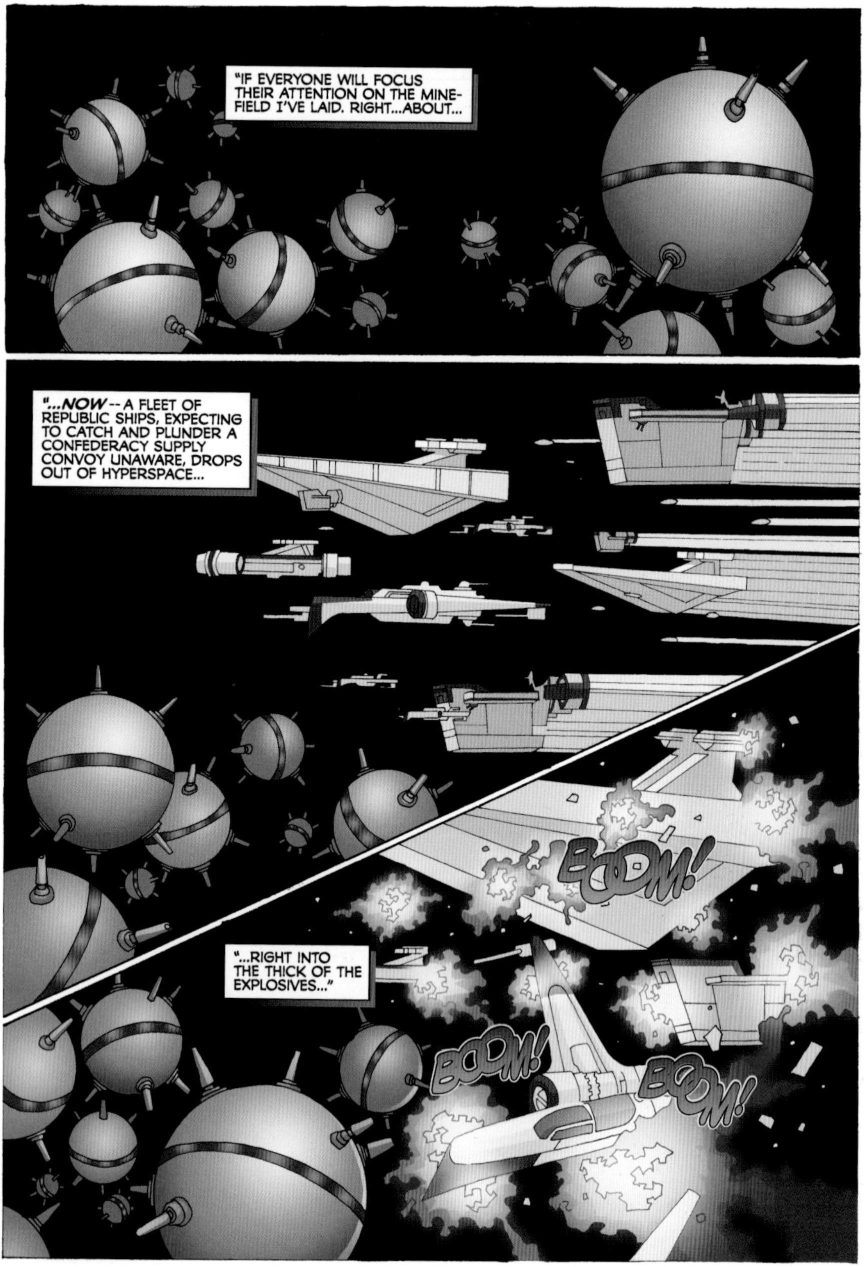
"IF EVERYONE WILL FOCUS THEIR ATTENTION ON THE MINE-FIELD I'VE LAID. RIGHT...ABOUT...
"...*NOW*-- A FLEET OF REPUBLIC SHIPS, EXPECTING TO CATCH AND PLUNDER A CONFEDERACY SUPPLY CONVOY UNAWARE, DROPS OUT OF HYPERSPACE...
BOOM!
"...RIGHT INTO THE THICK OF THE EXPLOSIVES..."
BOOM!
BOOM!

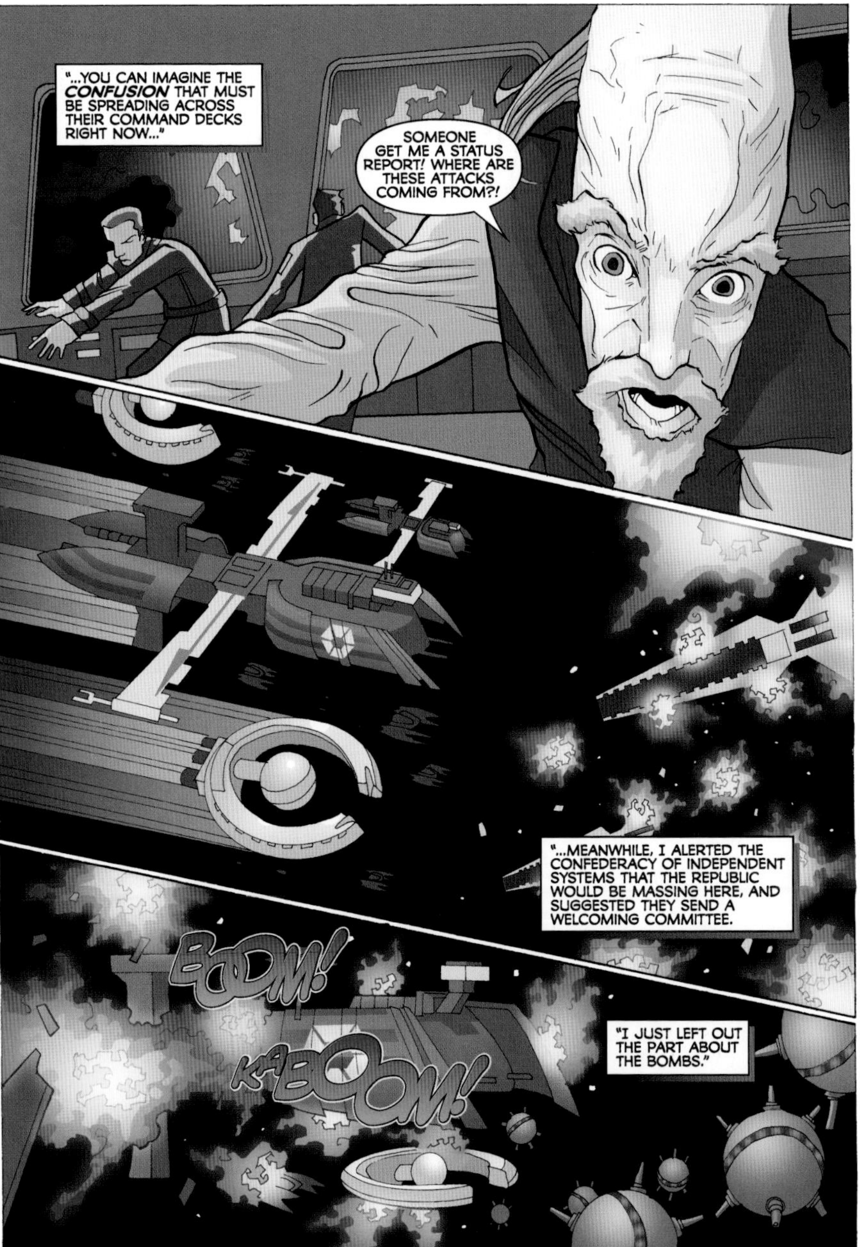
"...YOU CAN IMAGINE THE CONFUSION THAT MUST BE SPREADING ACROSS THEIR COMMAND DECKS RIGHT NOW..."
SOMEONE GET ME A STATUS REPORT! WHERE ARE THESE ATTACKS COMING FROM?!
"...MEANWHILE, I ALERTED THE CONFEDERACY OF INDEPENDENT SYSTEMS THAT THE REPUBLIC WOULD BE MASSING HERE, AND SUGGESTED THEY SEND A WELCOMING COMMITTEE.
BOOM!
KABOOM!
"I JUST LEFT OUT THE PART ABOUT THE BOMBS."

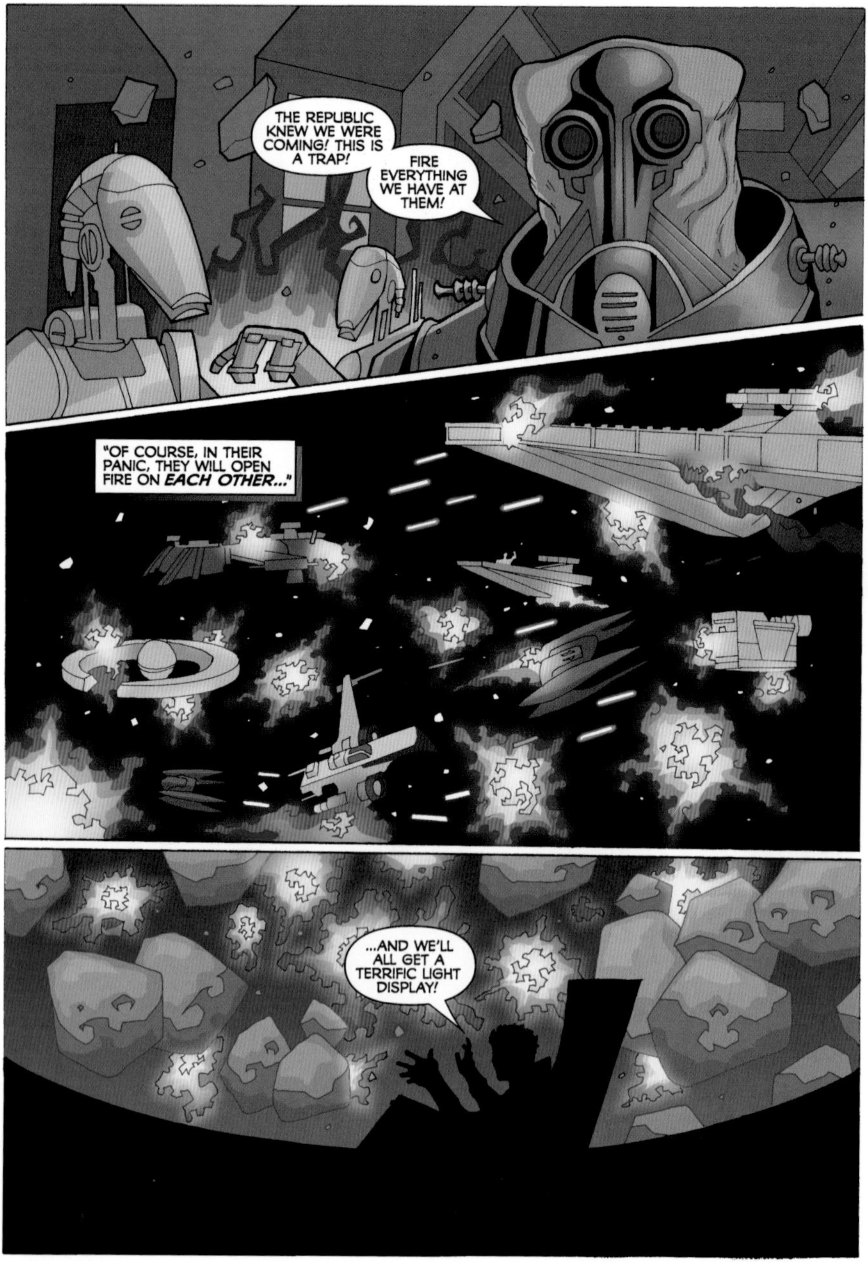
THE REPUBLIC KNEW WE WERE COMING! THIS IS A TRAP!
FIRE EVERYTHING WE HAVE AT THEM!
"OF COURSE, IN THEIR PANIC, THEY WILL OPEN FIRE ON *EACH OTHER*..."
...AND WE'LL ALL GET A TERRIFIC LIGHT DISPLAY!

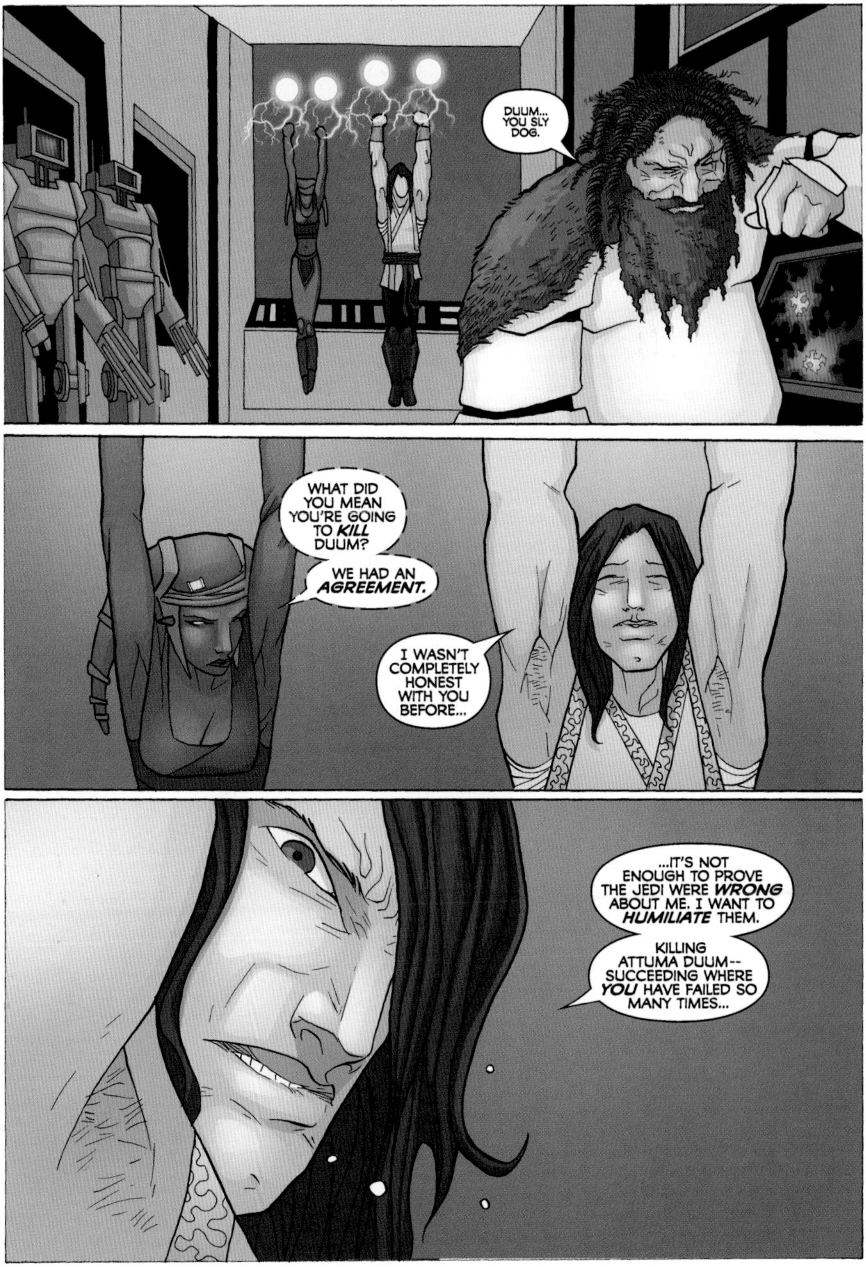
DUUM... YOU SLY DOG.
WHAT DID YOU MEAN YOU'RE GOING TO *KILL* DUUM?
WE HAD AN *AGREEMENT.*
I WASN'T COMPLETELY HONEST WITH YOU BEFORE...
...IT'S NOT ENOUGH TO PROVE THE JEDI WERE *WRONG* ABOUT ME. I WANT TO *HUMILIATE* THEM.
KILLING ATTUMA DUUM-- SUCCEEDING WHERE *YOU* HAVE FAILED SO MANY TIMES...

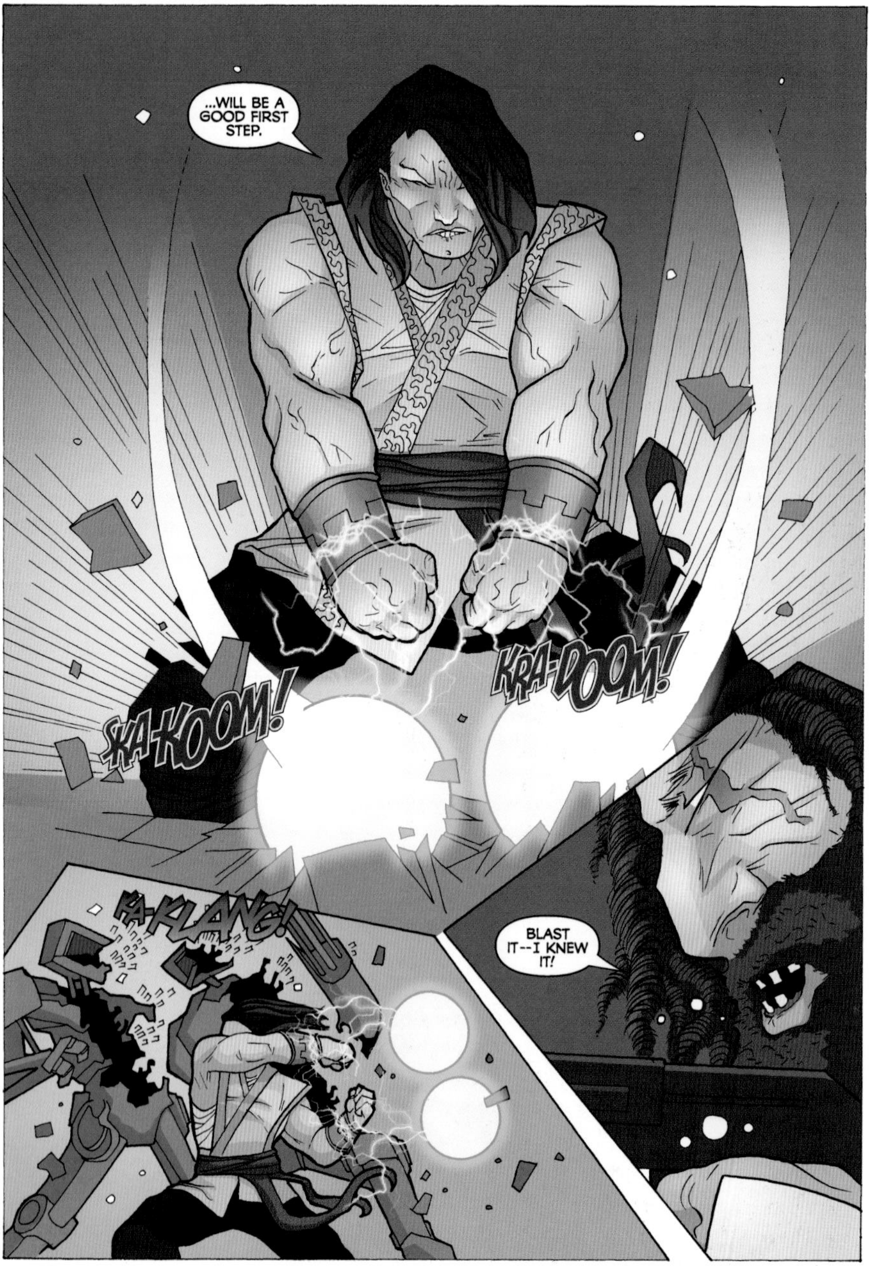
...WILL BE A GOOD FIRST STEP.
KRA-DOOM!
SKA-KOOM!
KA-KLANG!
BLAST IT--I KNEW IT!

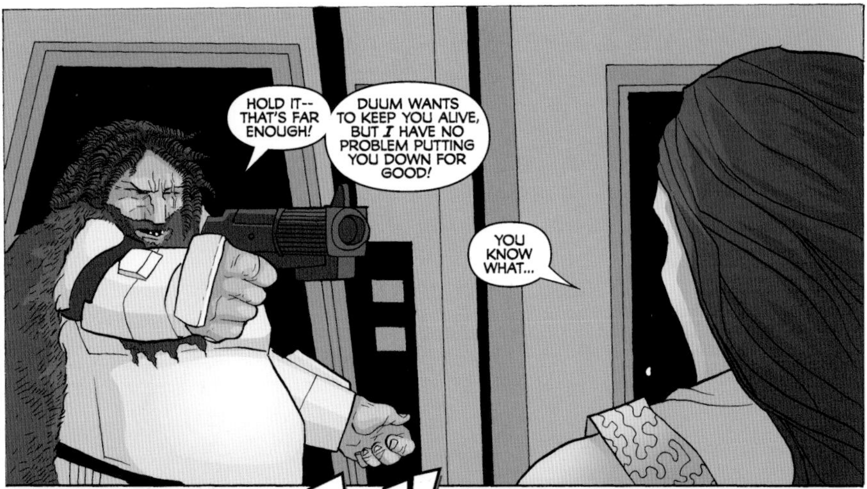
HOLD IT--
THAT'S FAR ENOUGH!
DUUM WANTS TO KEEP YOU ALIVE, BUT *I* HAVE NO PROBLEM PUTTING YOU DOWN FOR GOOD!
YOU KNOW WHAT...

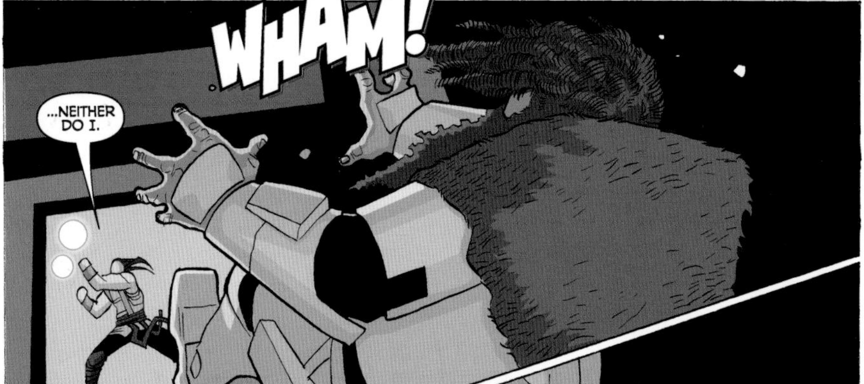
WHAM!
...NEITHER DO I.

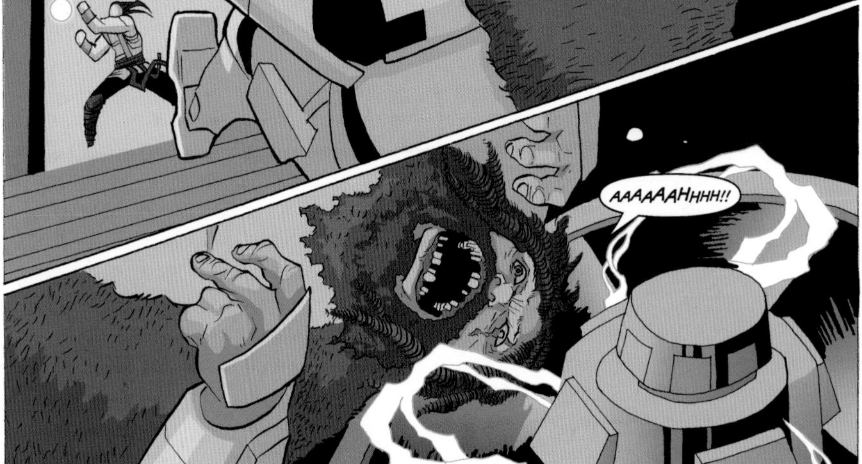
AAAAAAHHHH!!

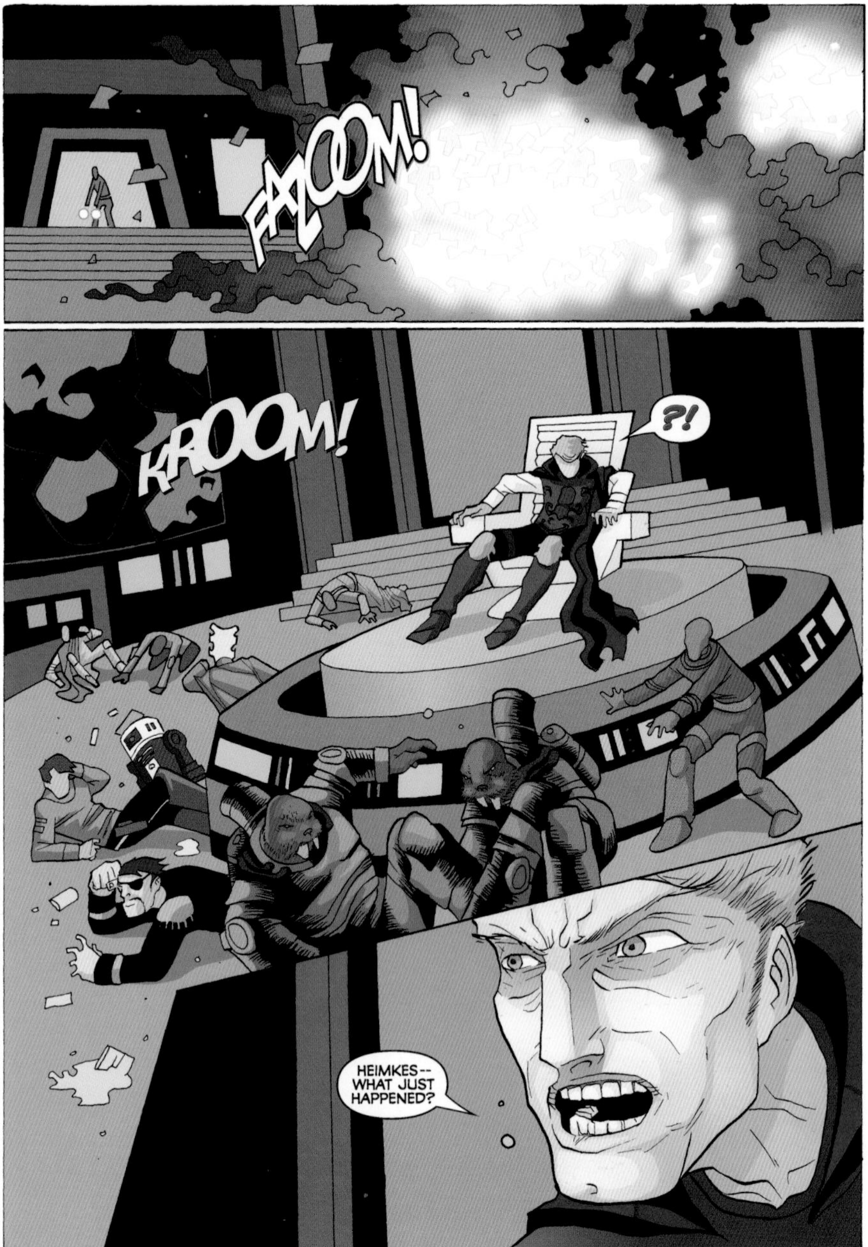
FAZOOM!
KROOM!
?!
HEIMKES--
WHAT JUST
HAPPENED?

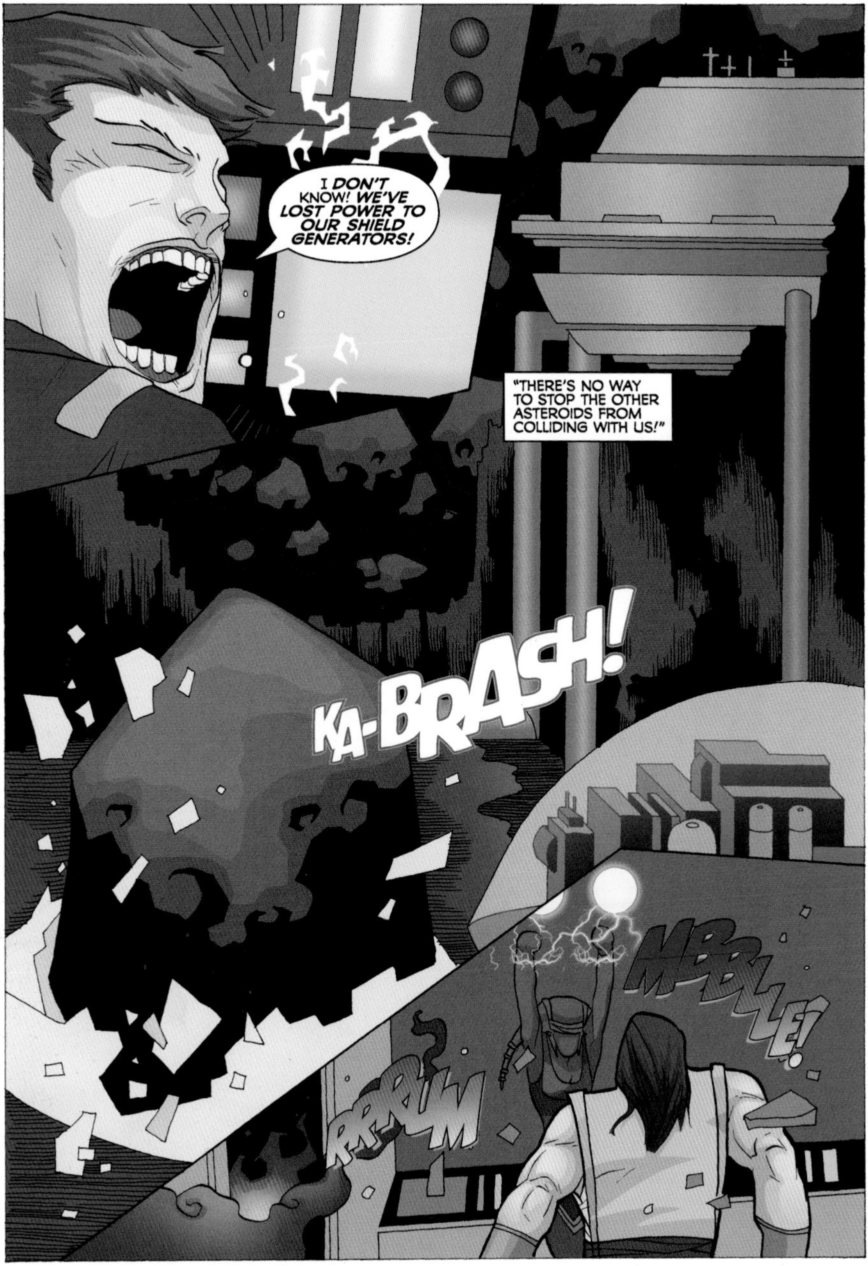

I DON'T KNOW! WE'VE LOST POWER TO OUR SHIELD GENERATORS!
"THERE'S NO WAY TO STOP THE OTHER ASTEROIDS FROM COLLIDING WITH US!"
KA-BRASH!
MBBLE!
RRRUM

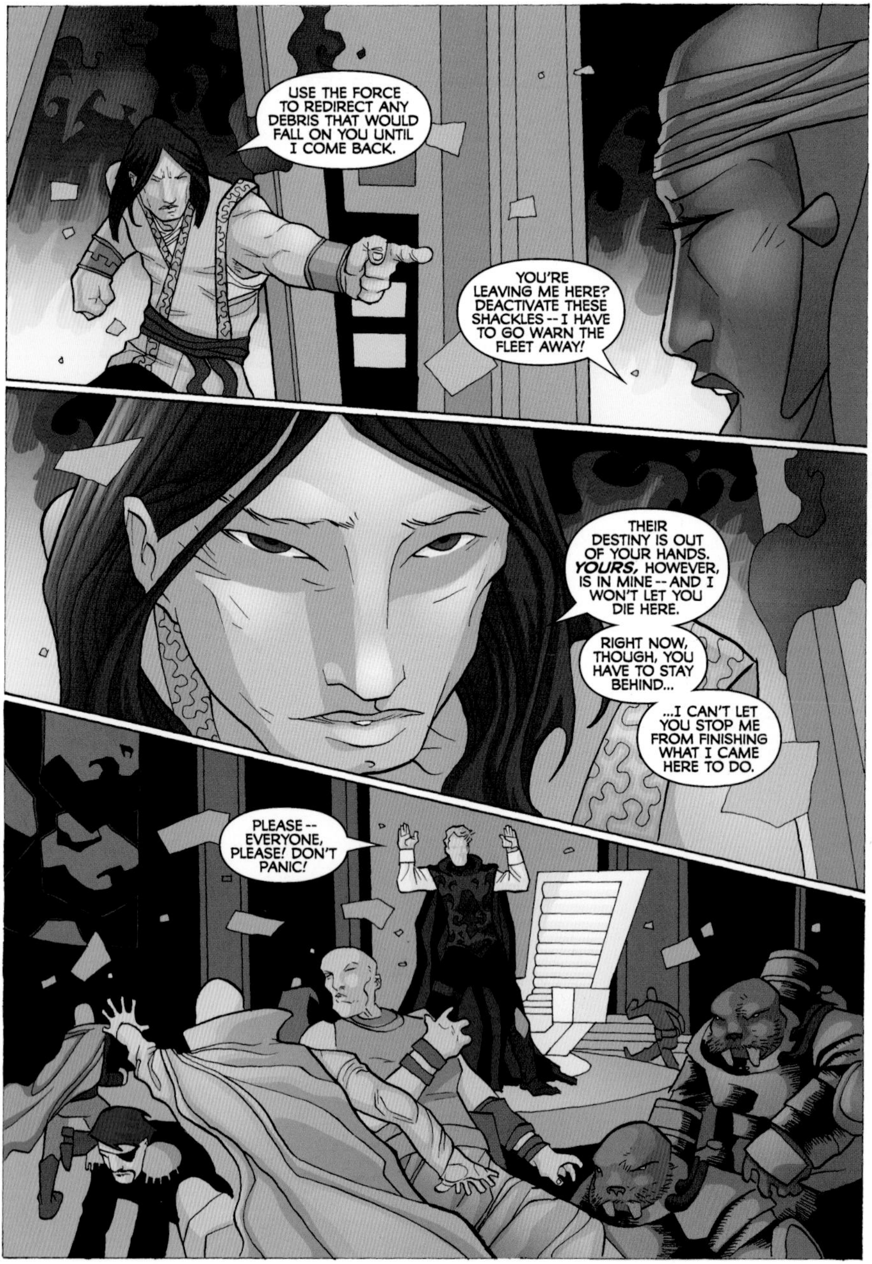

USE THE FORCE TO REDIRECT ANY DEBRIS THAT WOULD FALL ON YOU UNTIL I COME BACK.
YOU'RE LEAVING ME HERE? DEACTIVATE THESE SHACKLES -- I HAVE TO GO WARN THE FLEET AWAY!
THEIR DESTINY IS OUT OF YOUR HANDS. ***YOURS,*** HOWEVER, IS IN MINE -- AND I WON'T LET YOU DIE HERE.
RIGHT NOW, THOUGH, YOU HAVE TO STAY BEHIND...
...I CAN'T LET YOU STOP ME FROM FINISHING WHAT I CAME HERE TO DO.
PLEASE -- EVERYONE, PLEASE! DON'T PANIC!

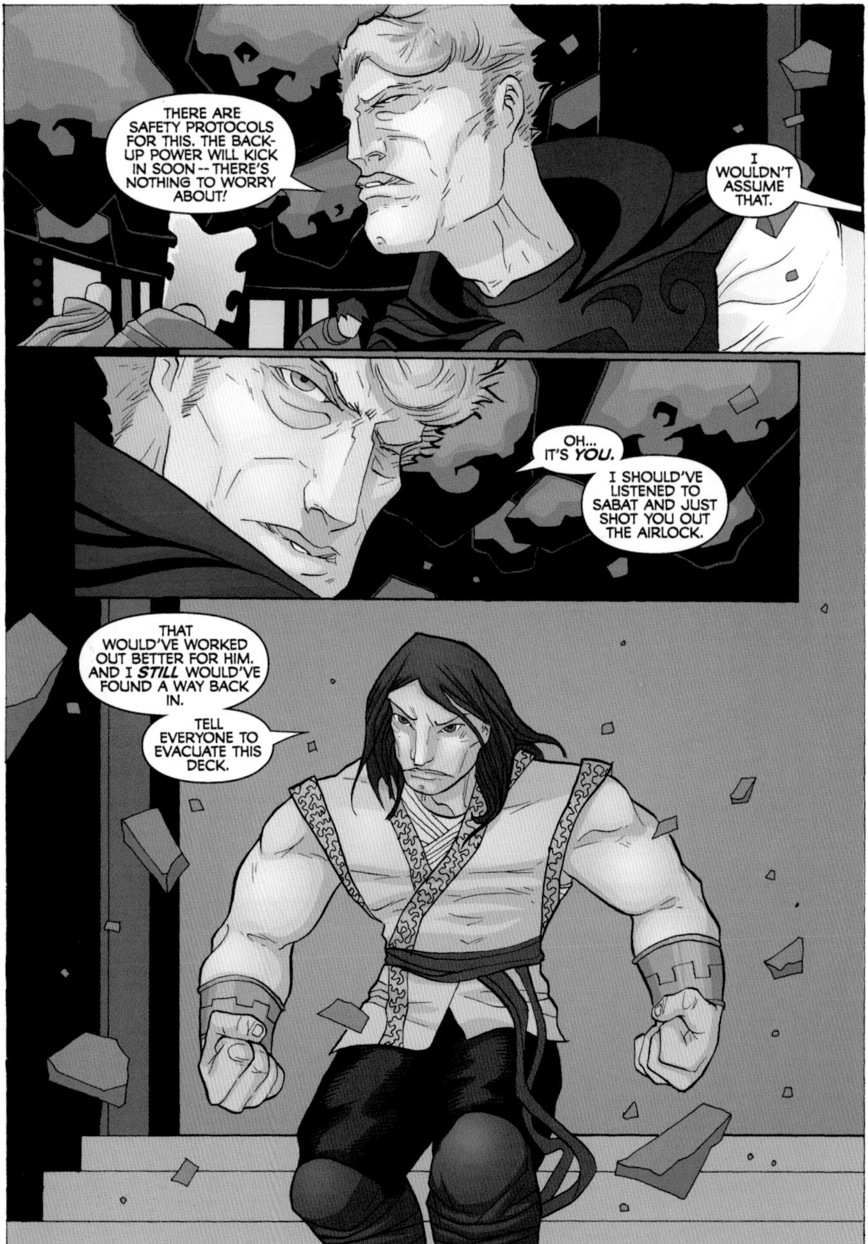
THERE ARE SAFETY PROTOCOLS FOR THIS. THE BACK-UP POWER WILL KICK IN SOON -- THERE'S NOTHING TO WORRY ABOUT!
I WOULDN'T ASSUME THAT.
OH... IT'S *YOU.*
I SHOULD'VE LISTENED TO SABAT AND JUST SHOT YOU OUT THE AIRLOCK.
THAT WOULD'VE WORKED OUT BETTER FOR HIM. AND I *STILL* WOULD'VE FOUND A WAY BACK IN.
TELL EVERYONE TO EVACUATE THIS DECK.

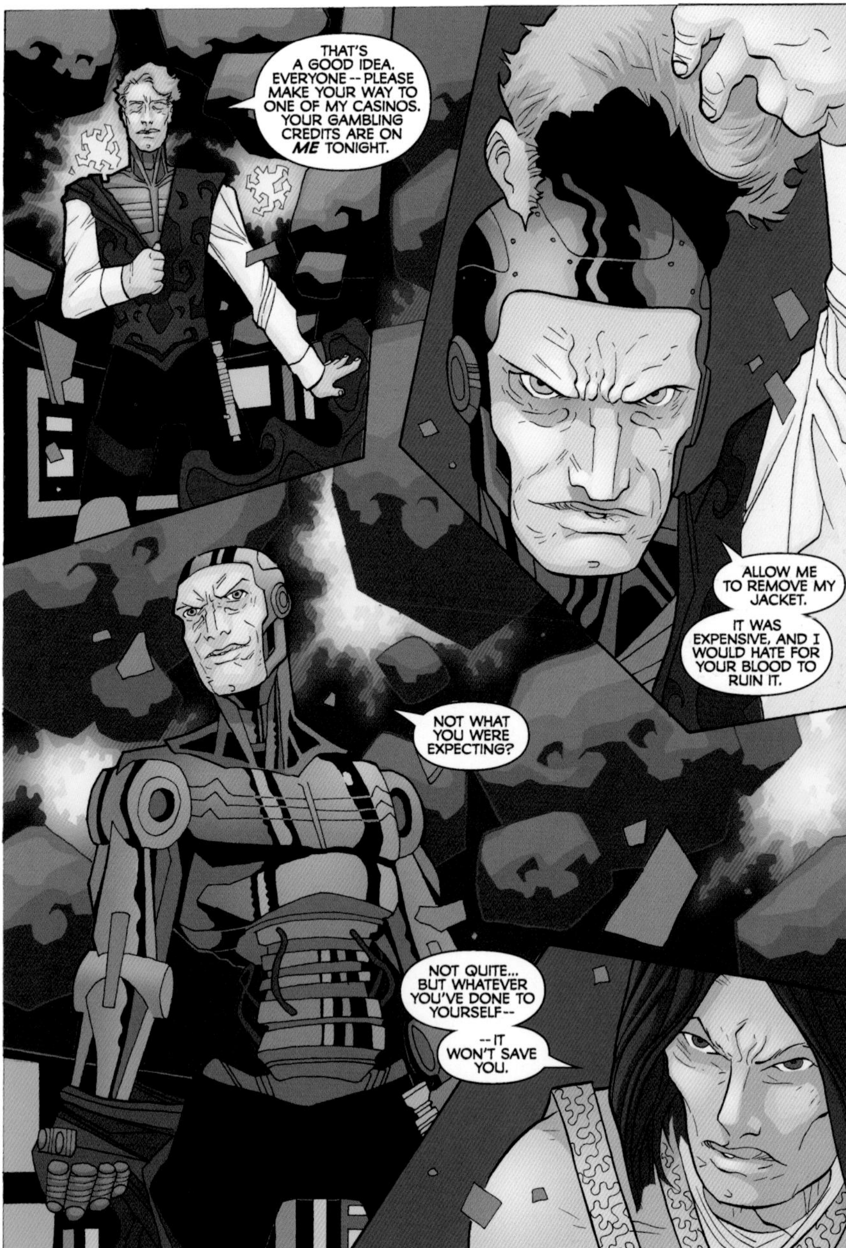
THAT'S A GOOD IDEA. EVERYONE -- PLEASE MAKE YOUR WAY TO ONE OF MY CASINOS. YOUR GAMBLING CREDITS ARE ON *ME* TONIGHT.
ALLOW ME TO REMOVE MY JACKET.
IT WAS EXPENSIVE, AND I WOULD HATE FOR YOUR BLOOD TO RUIN IT.
NOT WHAT YOU WERE EXPECTING?
NOT QUITE... BUT WHATEVER YOU'VE DONE TO YOURSELF--
--IT WON'T SAVE YOU.

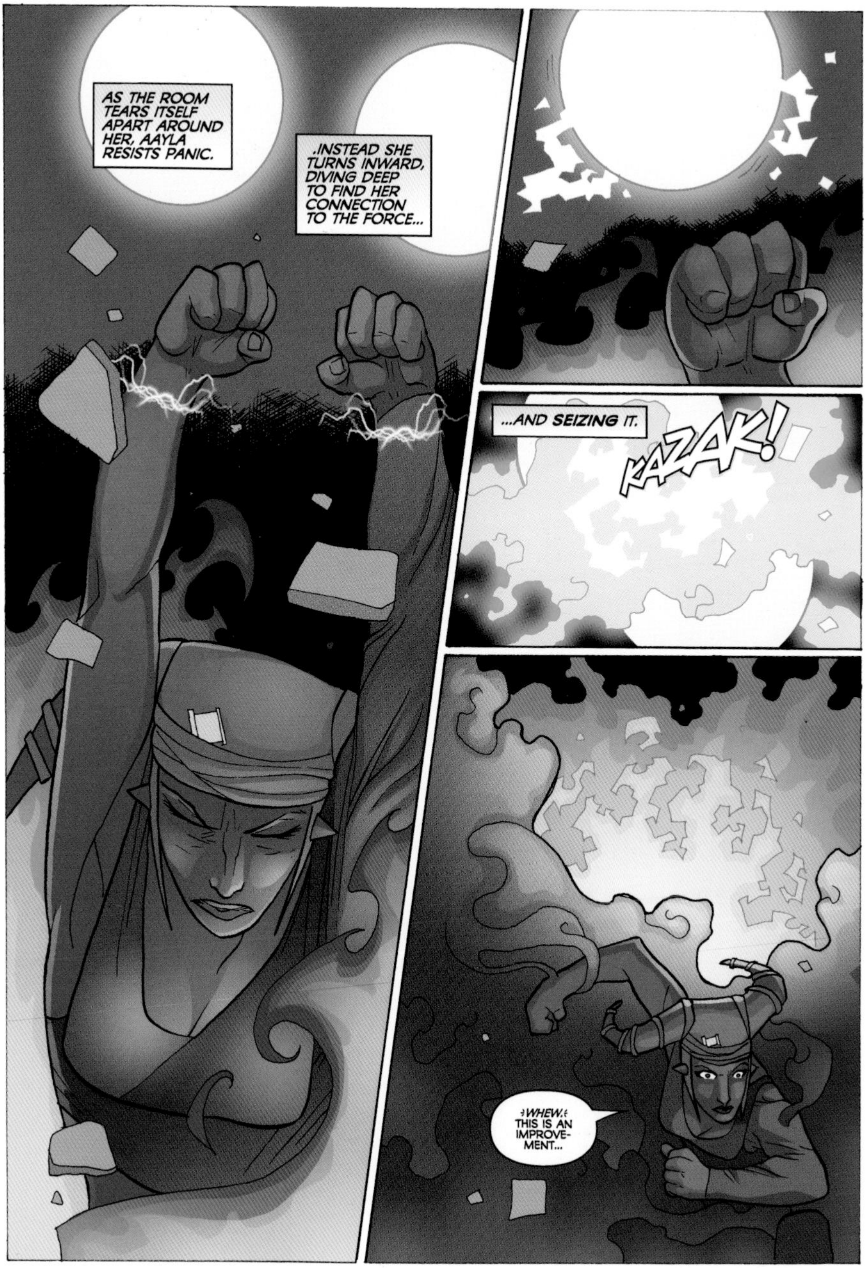
AS THE ROOM TEARS ITSELF APART AROUND HER, AAYLA RESISTS PANIC.
.INSTEAD SHE TURNS INWARD, DIVING DEEP TO FIND HER CONNECTION TO THE FORCE...
...AND SEIZING IT.
KAZAK!
WHEW. THIS IS AN IMPROVEMENT...

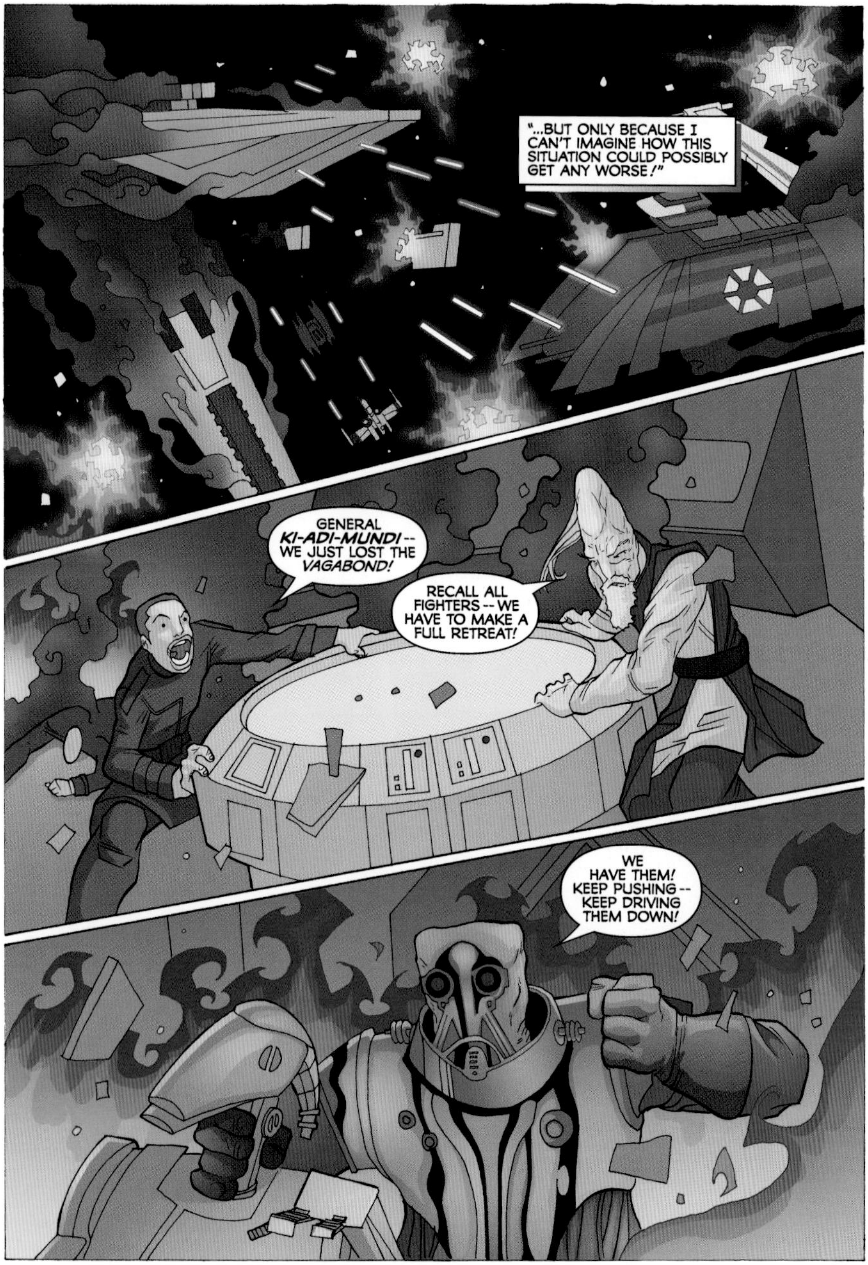

"...BUT ONLY BECAUSE I CAN'T IMAGINE HOW THIS SITUATION COULD POSSIBLY GET ANY WORSE!"
GENERAL KI-ADI-MUNDI -- WE JUST LOST THE VAGABOND!
RECALL ALL FIGHTERS -- WE HAVE TO MAKE A FULL RETREAT!
WE HAVE THEM! KEEP PUSHING -- KEEP DRIVING THEM DOWN!

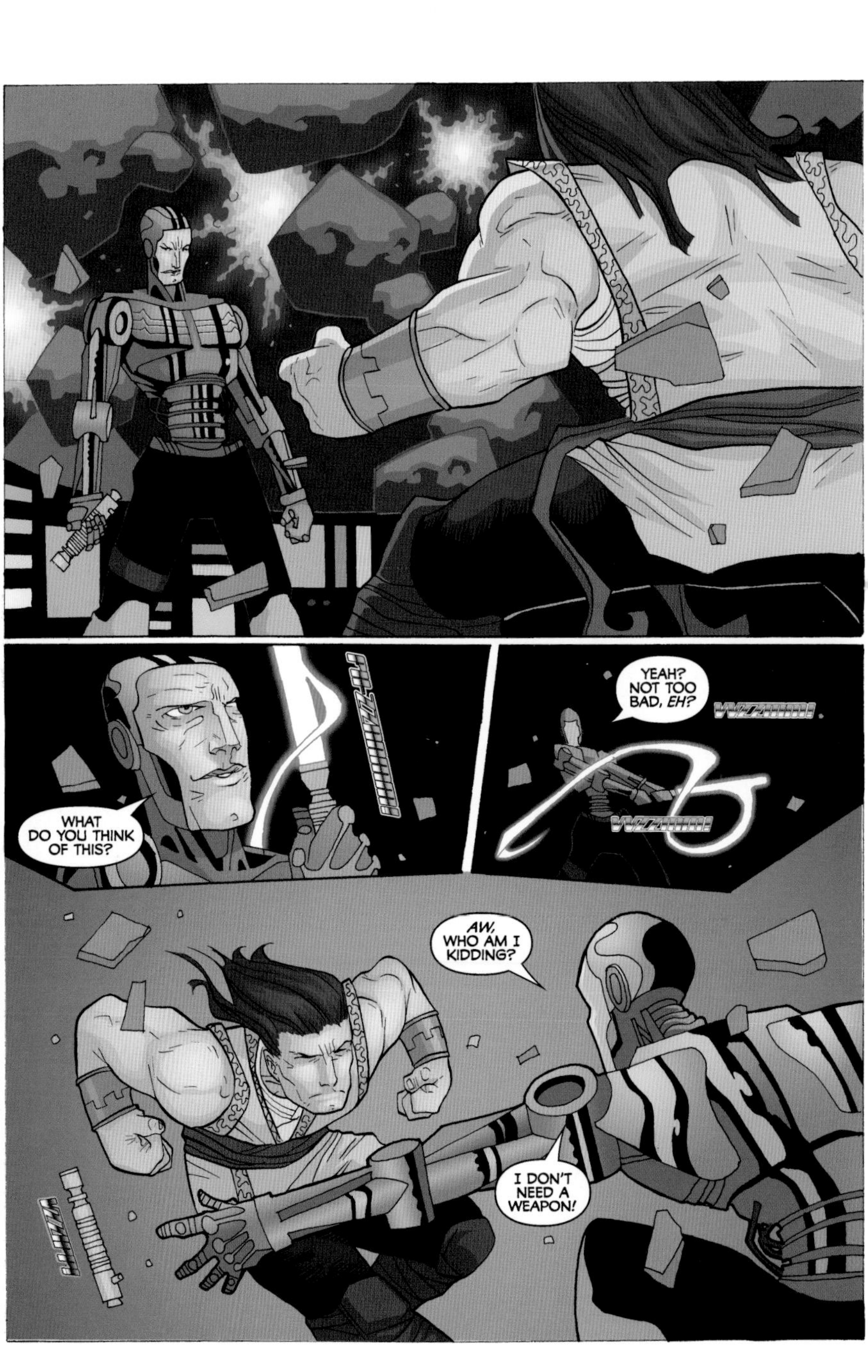
WHAT DO YOU THINK OF THIS?
YEAH? NOT TOO BAD, EH?
VVZZHMMM!
VVZZHMMM!
AW, WHO AM I KIDDING?
I DON'T NEED A WEAPON!

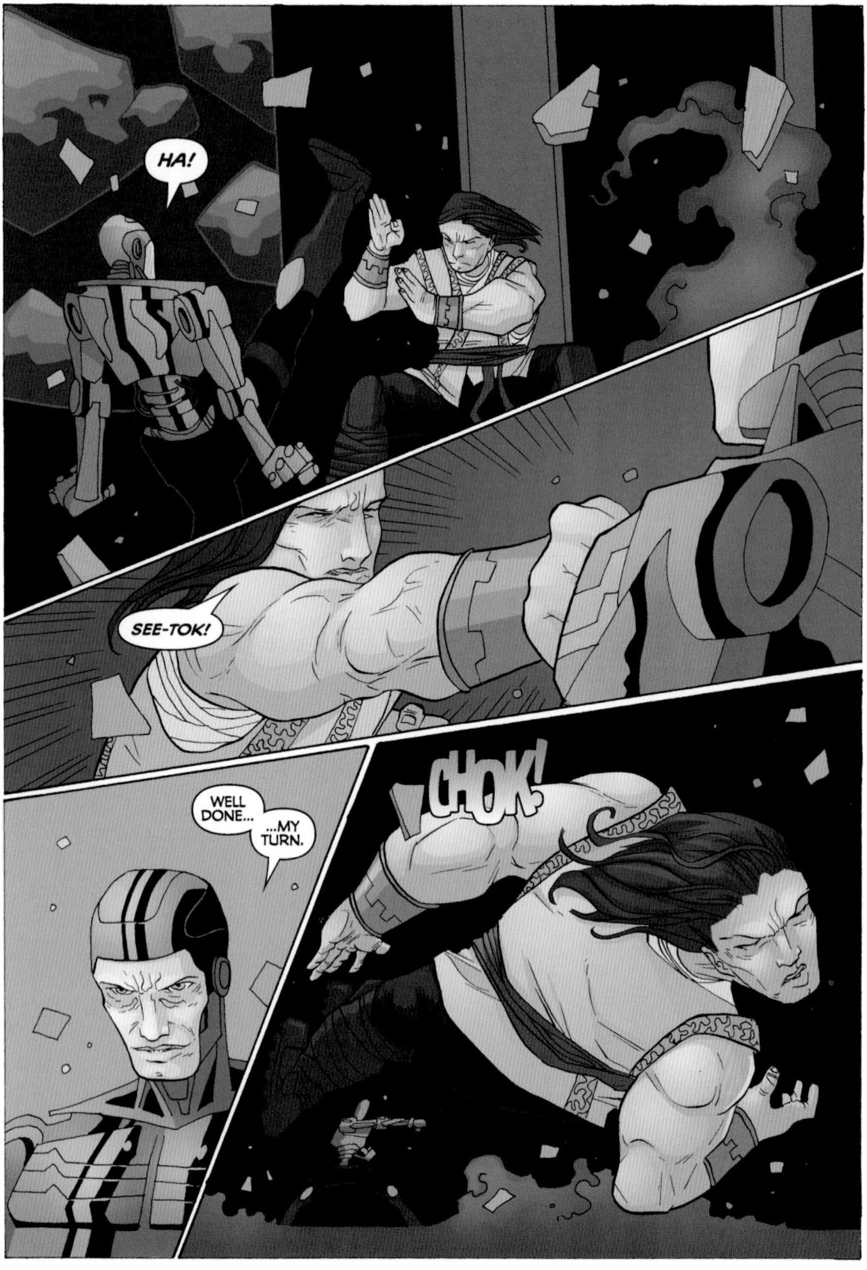
HA!
SEE-TOK!
WELL DONE...
...MY TURN.
CHOK!

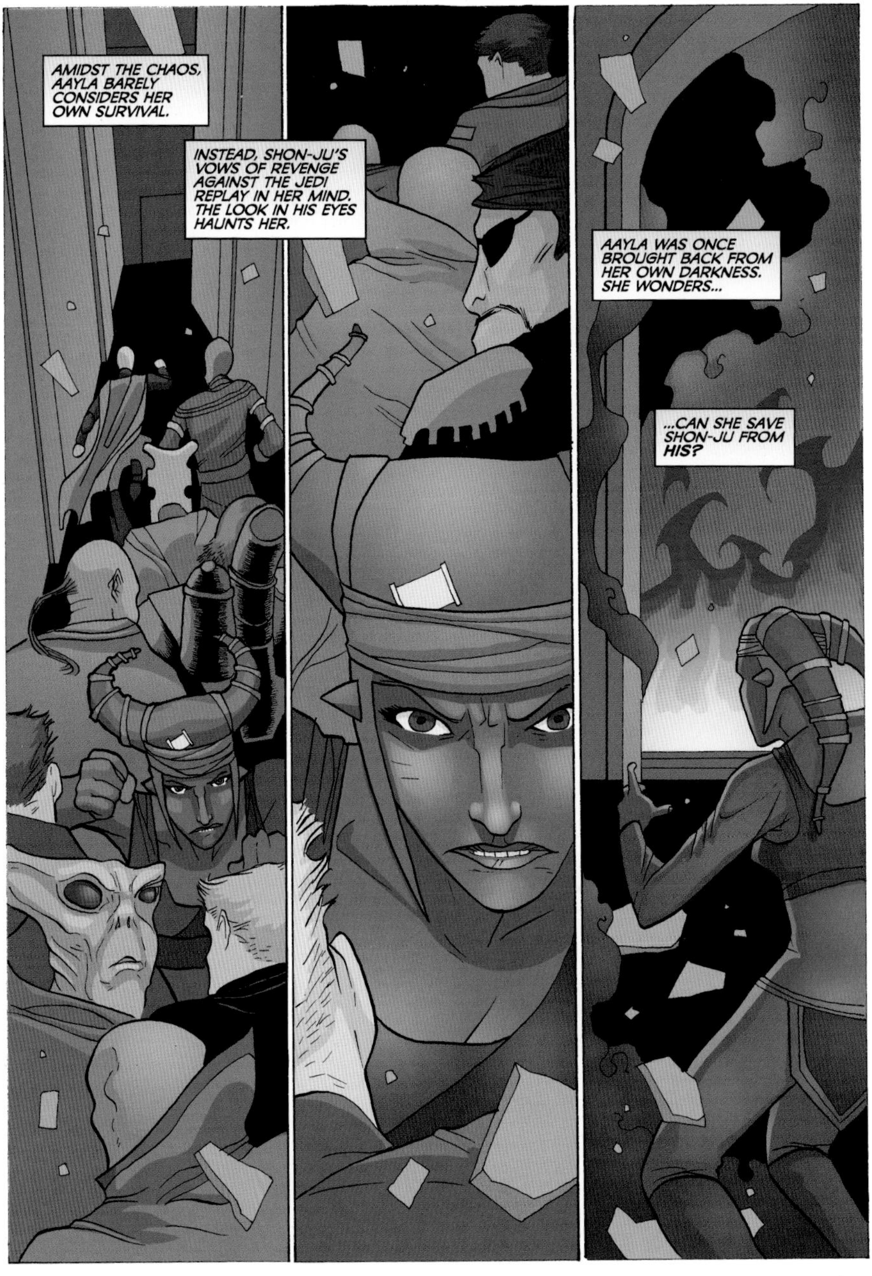
AMIDST THE CHAOS, AAYLA BARELY CONSIDERS HER OWN SURVIVAL.
INSTEAD, SHON-JU'S VOWS OF REVENGE AGAINST THE JEDI REPLAY IN HER MIND. THE LOOK IN HIS EYES HAUNTS HER.
AAYLA WAS ONCE BROUGHT BACK FROM HER OWN DARKNESS. SHE WONDERS...
...CAN SHE SAVE SHON-JU FROM **HIS?**

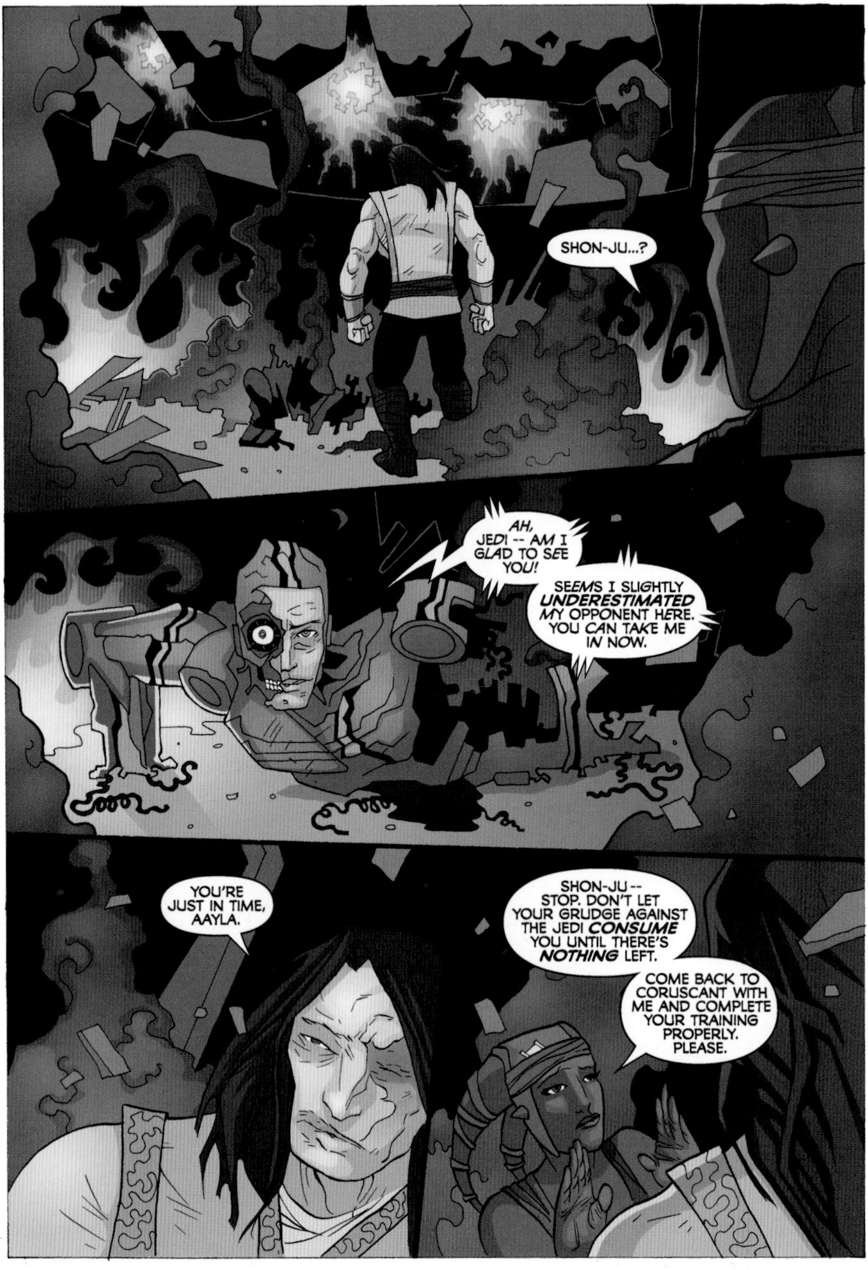
SHON-JU...?
AH, JEDI -- AM I GLAD TO SEE YOU!
SEEMS I SLIGHTLY UNDERESTIMATED MY OPPONENT HERE. YOU CAN TAKE ME IN NOW.
YOU'RE JUST IN TIME, AAYLA.
SHON-JU -- STOP. DON'T LET YOUR GRUDGE AGAINST THE JEDI CONSUME YOU UNTIL THERE'S NOTHING LEFT.
COME BACK TO CORUSCANT WITH ME AND COMPLETE YOUR TRAINING PROPERLY. PLEASE.

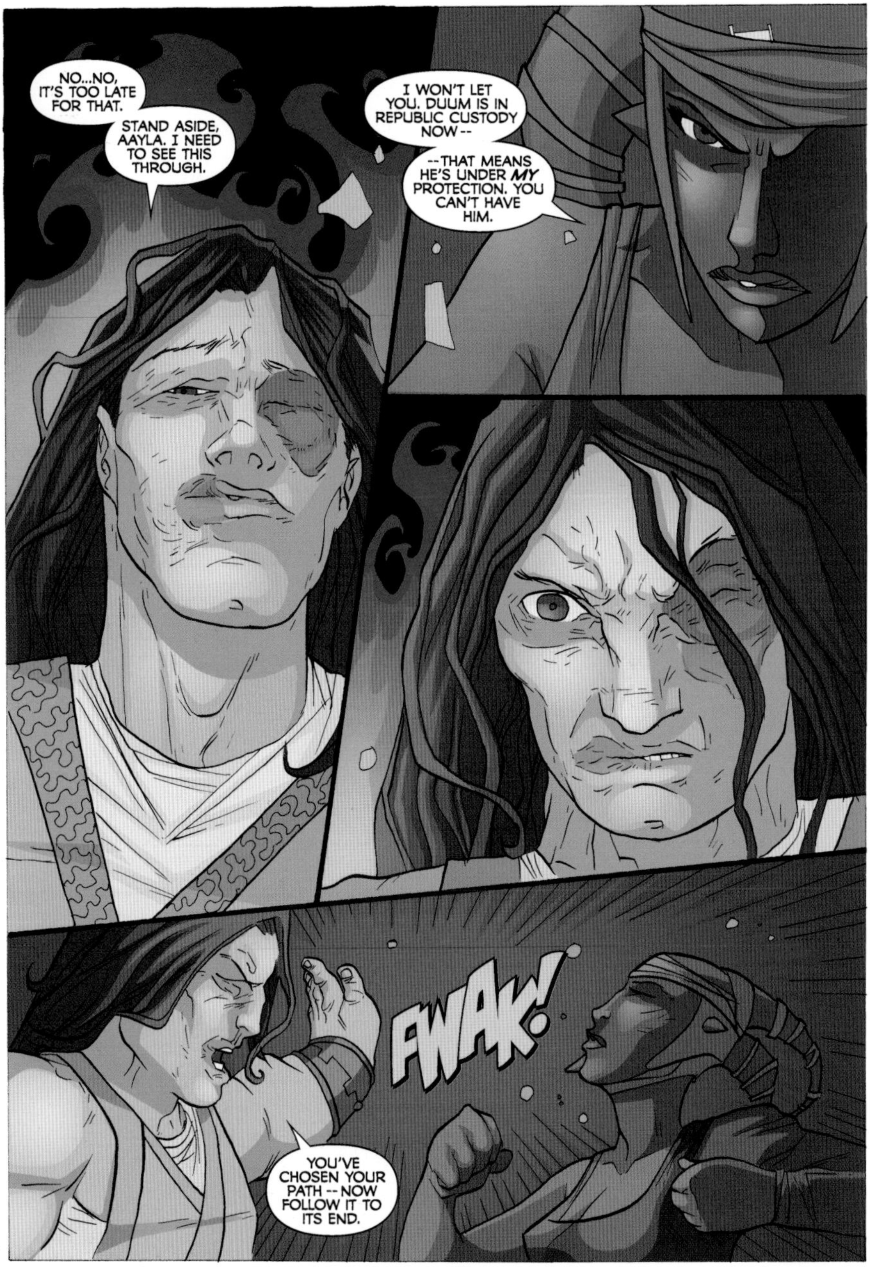
NO...NO, IT'S TOO LATE FOR THAT.
STAND ASIDE, AAYLA. I NEED TO SEE THIS THROUGH.
I WON'T LET YOU. DUUM IS IN REPUBLIC CUSTODY NOW --
--THAT MEANS HE'S UNDER *MY* PROTECTION. YOU CAN'T HAVE HIM.
FWAK!
YOU'VE CHOSEN YOUR PATH -- NOW FOLLOW IT TO ITS END.

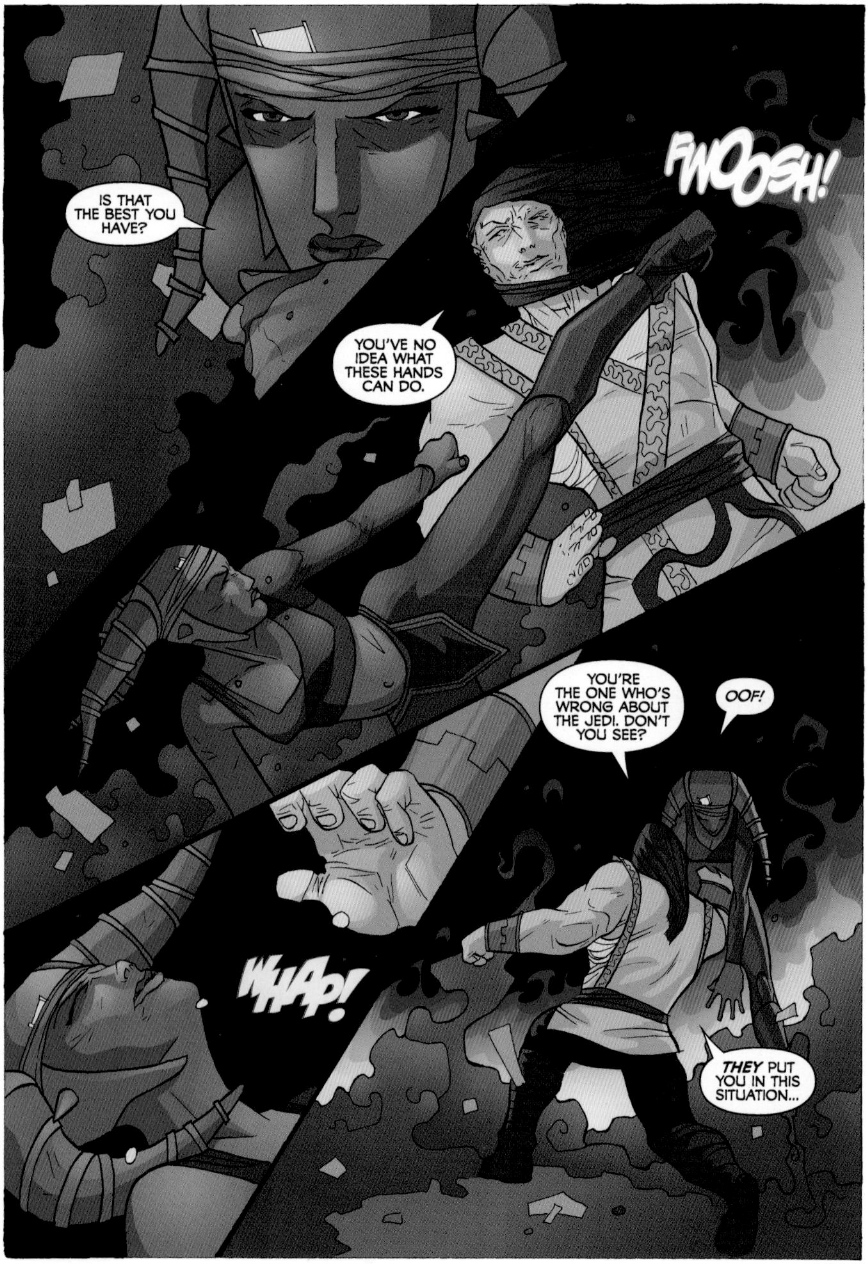
IS THAT THE BEST YOU HAVE?
FWOOSH!
YOU'VE NO IDEA WHAT THESE HANDS CAN DO.
YOU'RE THE ONE WHO'S WRONG ABOUT THE JEDI. DON'T YOU SEE?
OOF!
WHAP!
THEY PUT YOU IN THIS SITUATION...

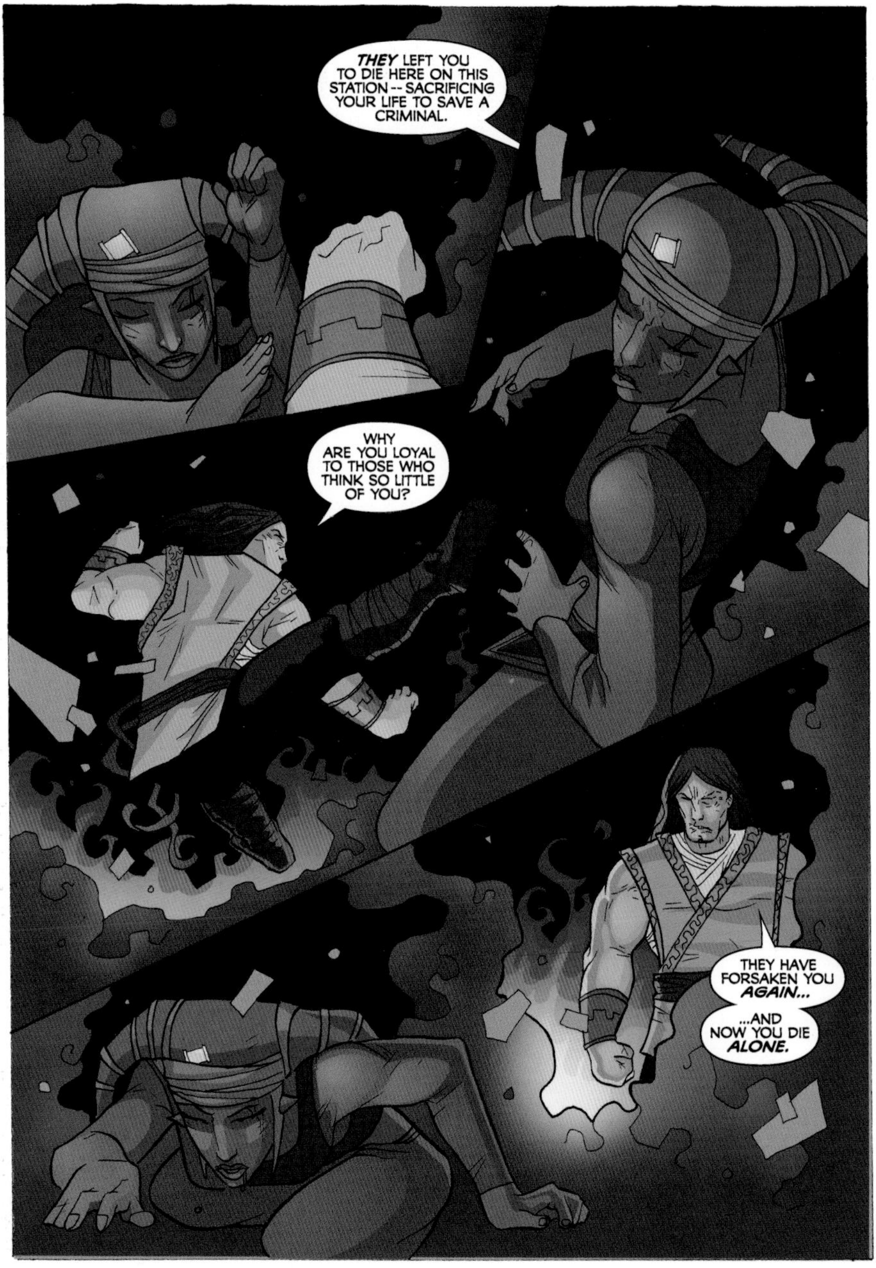

THEY LEFT YOU TO DIE HERE ON THIS STATION -- SACRIFICING YOUR LIFE TO SAVE A CRIMINAL.
WHY ARE YOU LOYAL TO THOSE WHO THINK SO LITTLE OF YOU?
THEY HAVE FORSAKEN YOU ***AGAIN...***
...AND NOW YOU DIE ***ALONE.***

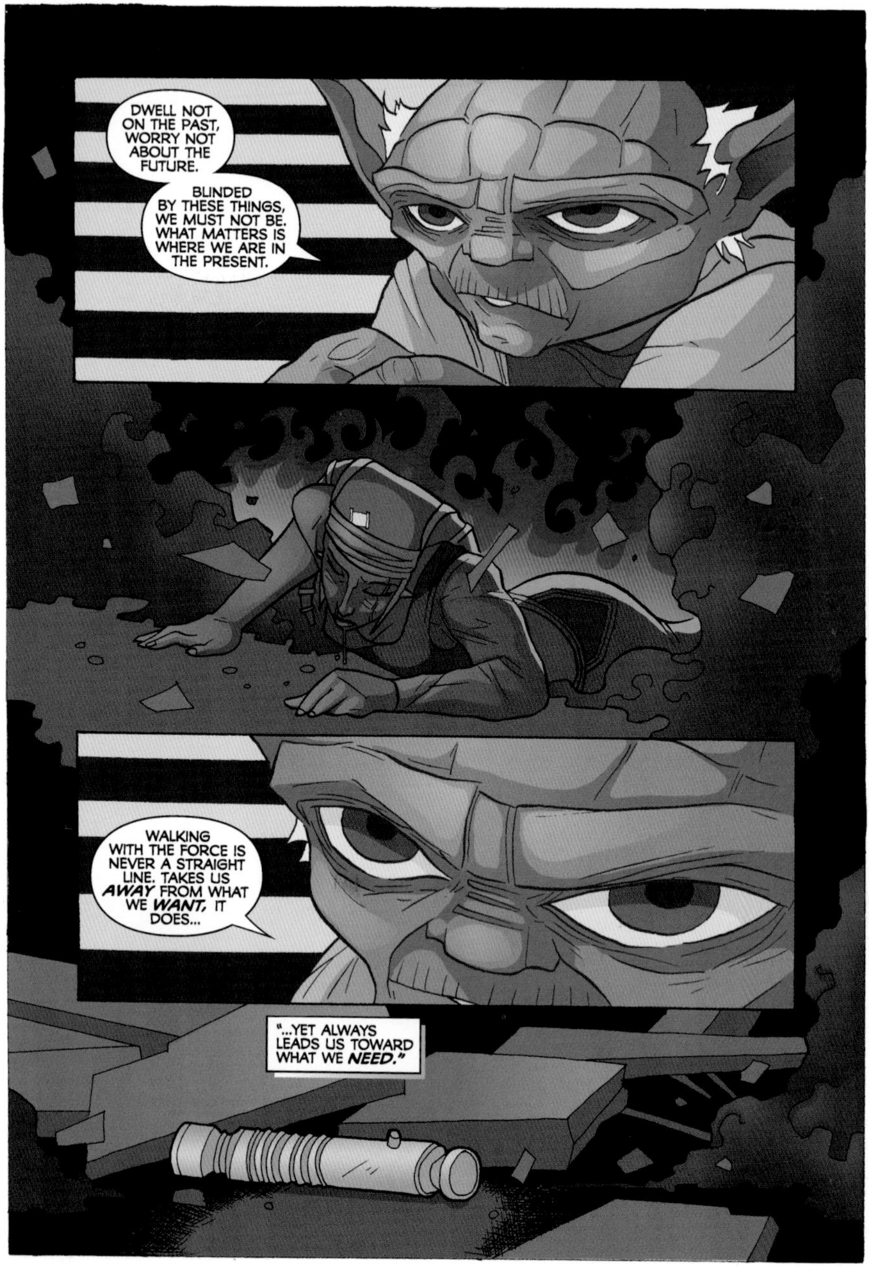

DWELL NOT ON THE PAST, WORRY NOT ABOUT THE FUTURE.
BLINDED BY THESE THINGS, WE MUST NOT BE. WHAT MATTERS IS WHERE WE ARE IN THE PRESENT.
WALKING WITH THE FORCE IS NEVER A STRAIGHT LINE. TAKES US AWAY FROM WHAT WE WANT, IT DOES...
"...YET ALWAYS LEADS US TOWARD WHAT WE NEED."

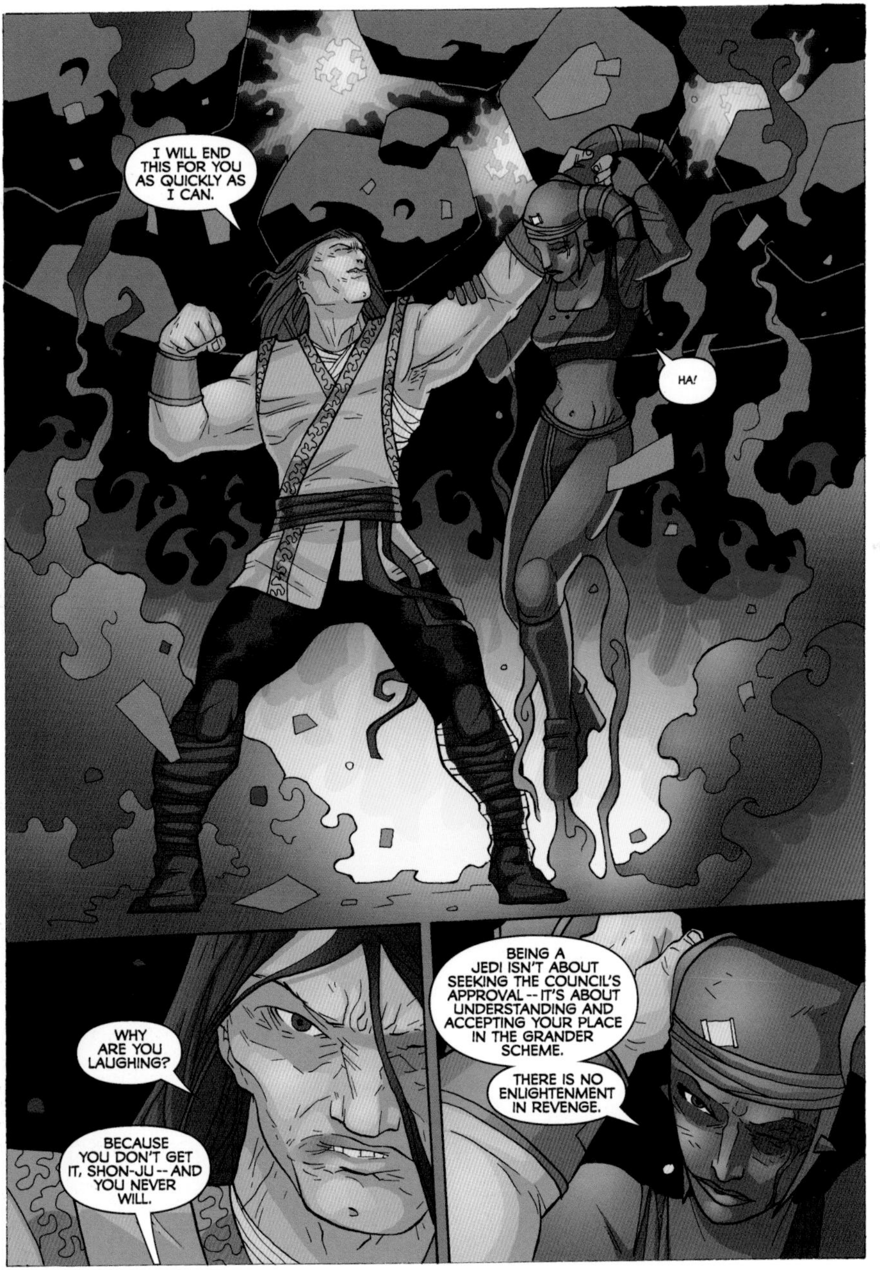
I WILL END THIS FOR YOU AS QUICKLY AS I CAN.
HA!
WHY ARE YOU LAUGHING?
BECAUSE YOU DON'T GET IT, SHON-JU -- AND YOU NEVER WILL.
BEING A JEDI ISN'T ABOUT SEEKING THE COUNCIL'S APPROVAL -- IT'S ABOUT UNDERSTANDING AND ACCEPTING YOUR PLACE IN THE GRANDER SCHEME.
THERE IS NO ENLIGHTENMENT IN REVENGE.

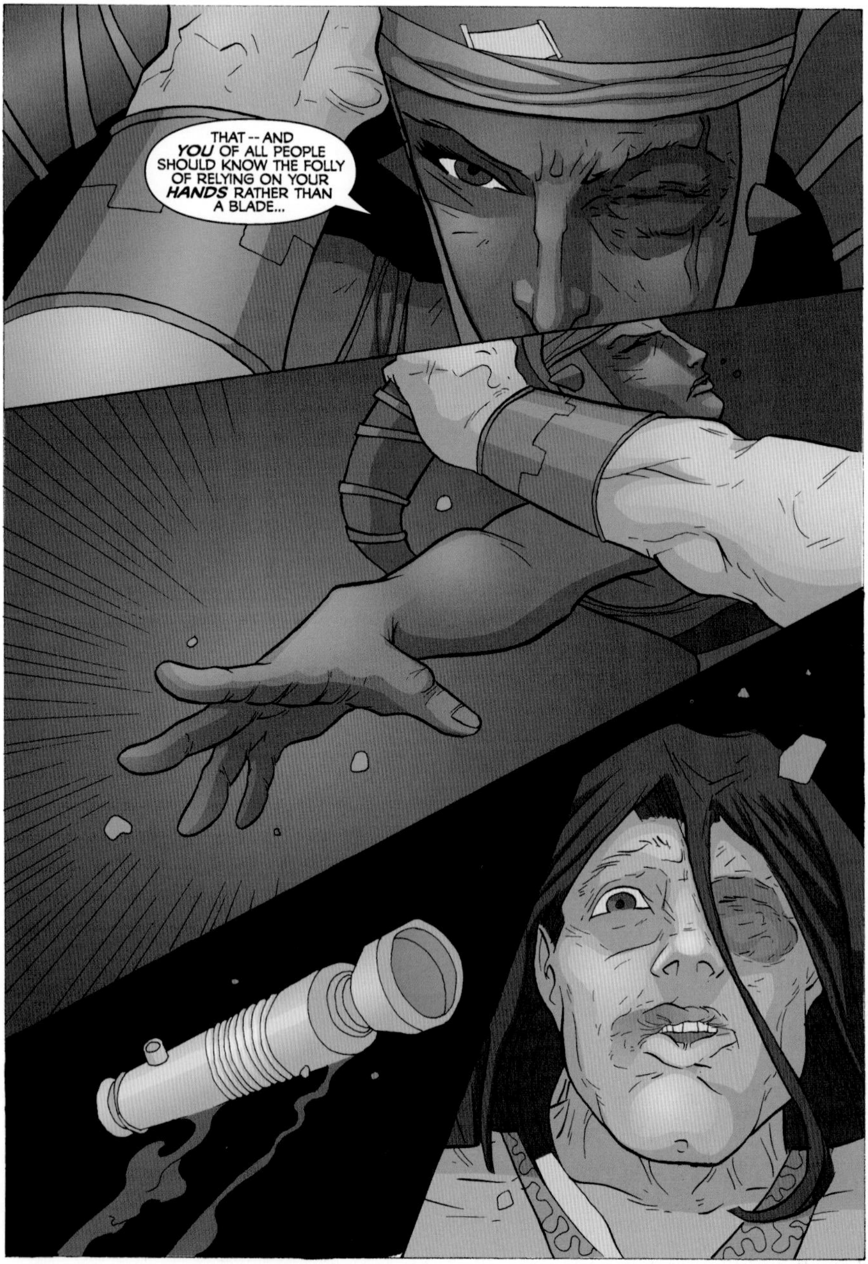
THAT -- AND *YOU* OF ALL PEOPLE SHOULD KNOW THE FOLLY OF RELYING ON YOUR *HANDS* RATHER THAN A BLADE...

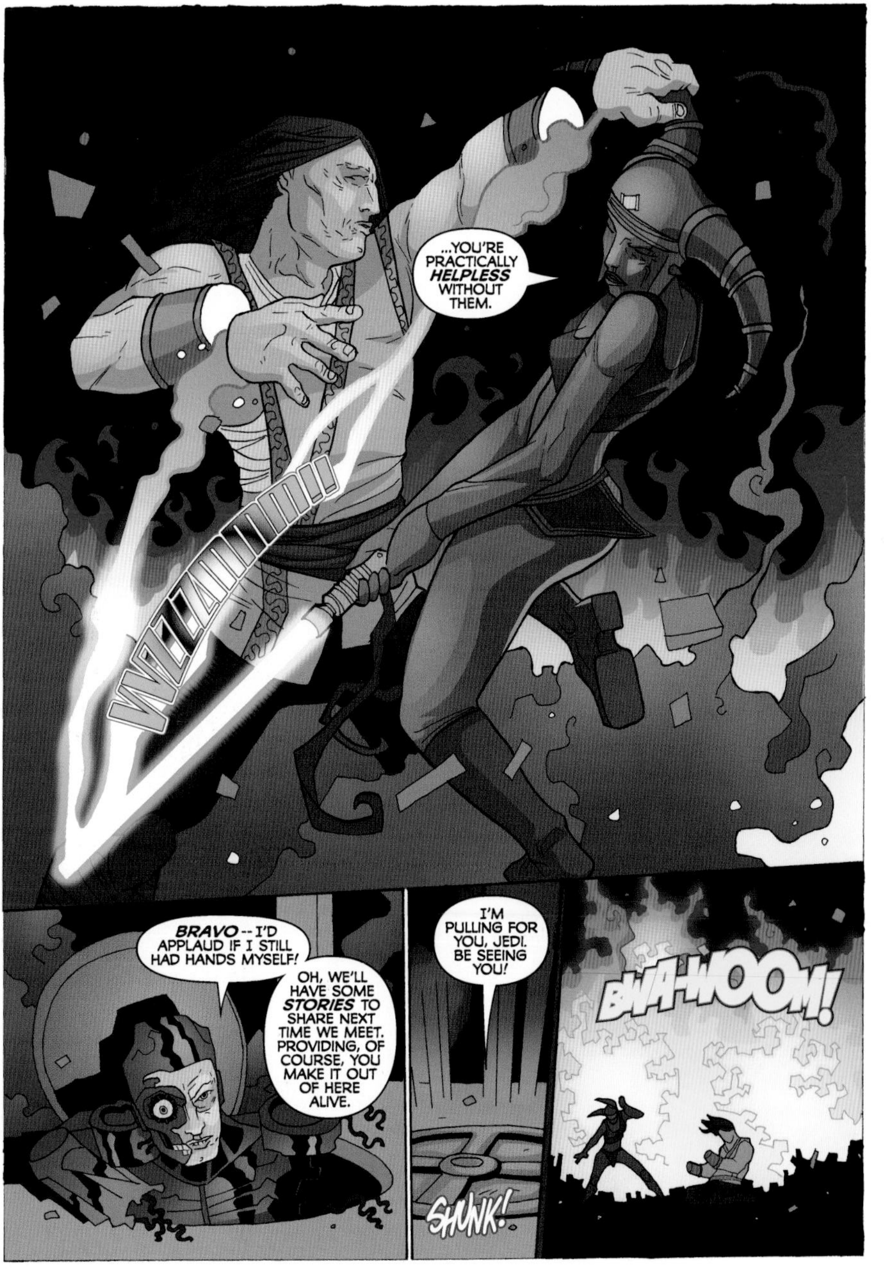
...YOU'RE PRACTICALLY HELPLESS WITHOUT THEM.
VVZZAAAMMM!!
BRAVO--I'D APPLAUD IF I STILL HAD HANDS MYSELF!
OH, WE'LL HAVE SOME STORIES TO SHARE NEXT TIME WE MEET. PROVIDING, OF COURSE, YOU MAKE IT OUT OF HERE ALIVE.
I'M PULLING FOR YOU, JEDI. BE SEEING YOU!
SHUNK!
BWA-WOOM!

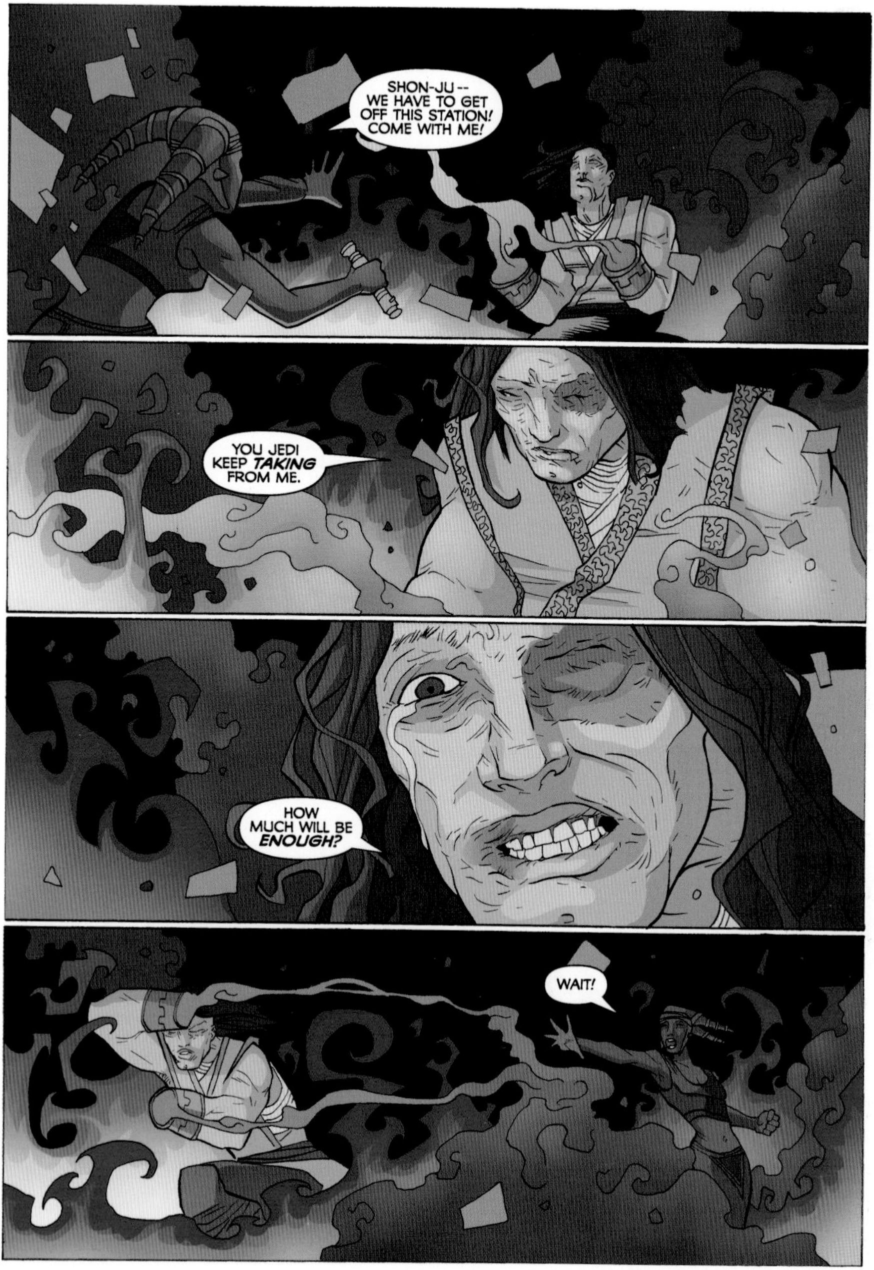
SHON-JU -- WE HAVE TO GET OFF THIS STATION! COME WITH ME!
YOU JEDI KEEP *TAKING* FROM ME.
HOW MUCH WILL BE *ENOUGH?*
WAIT!

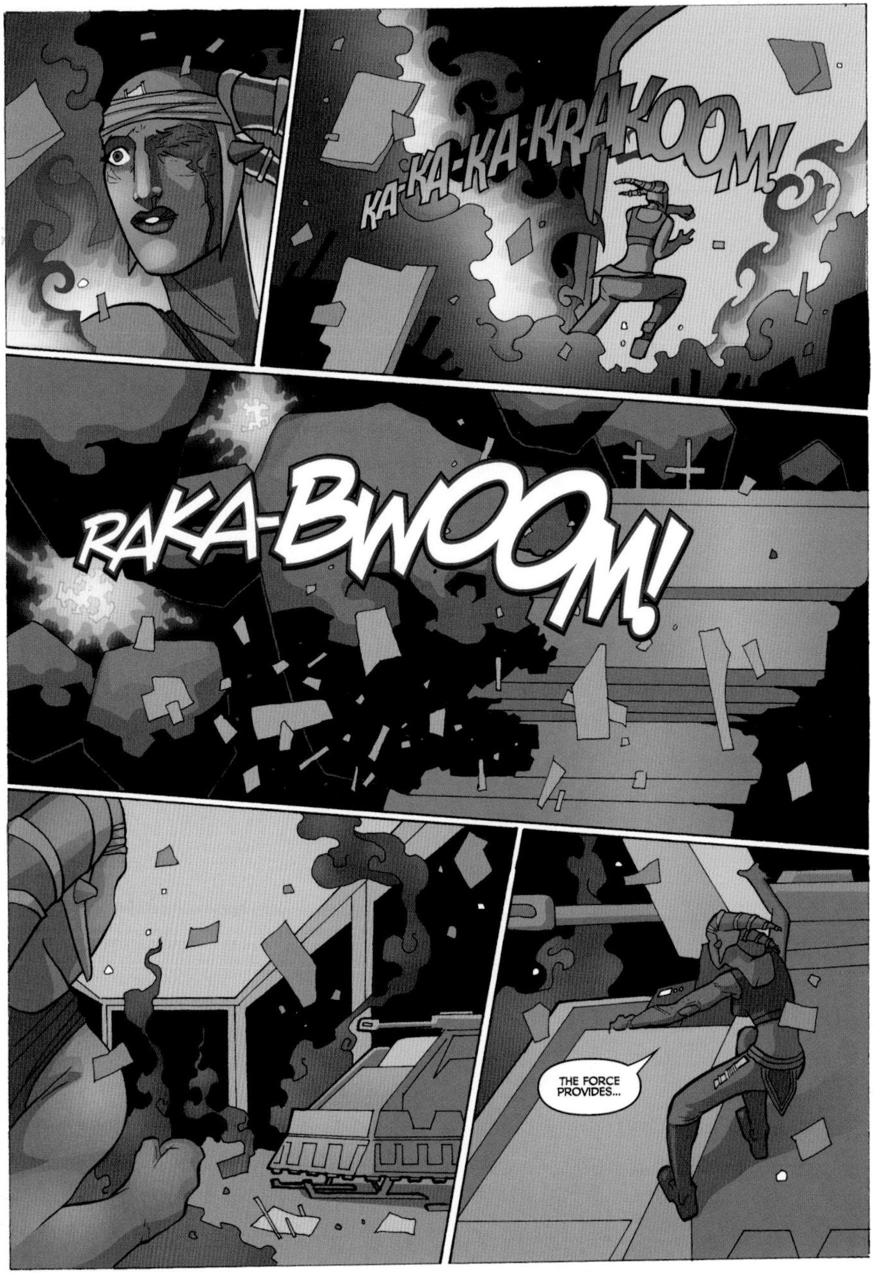
KA-KA-KA-KRAKOOM!
RAKA-BWOOOM!
THE FORCE PROVIDES...

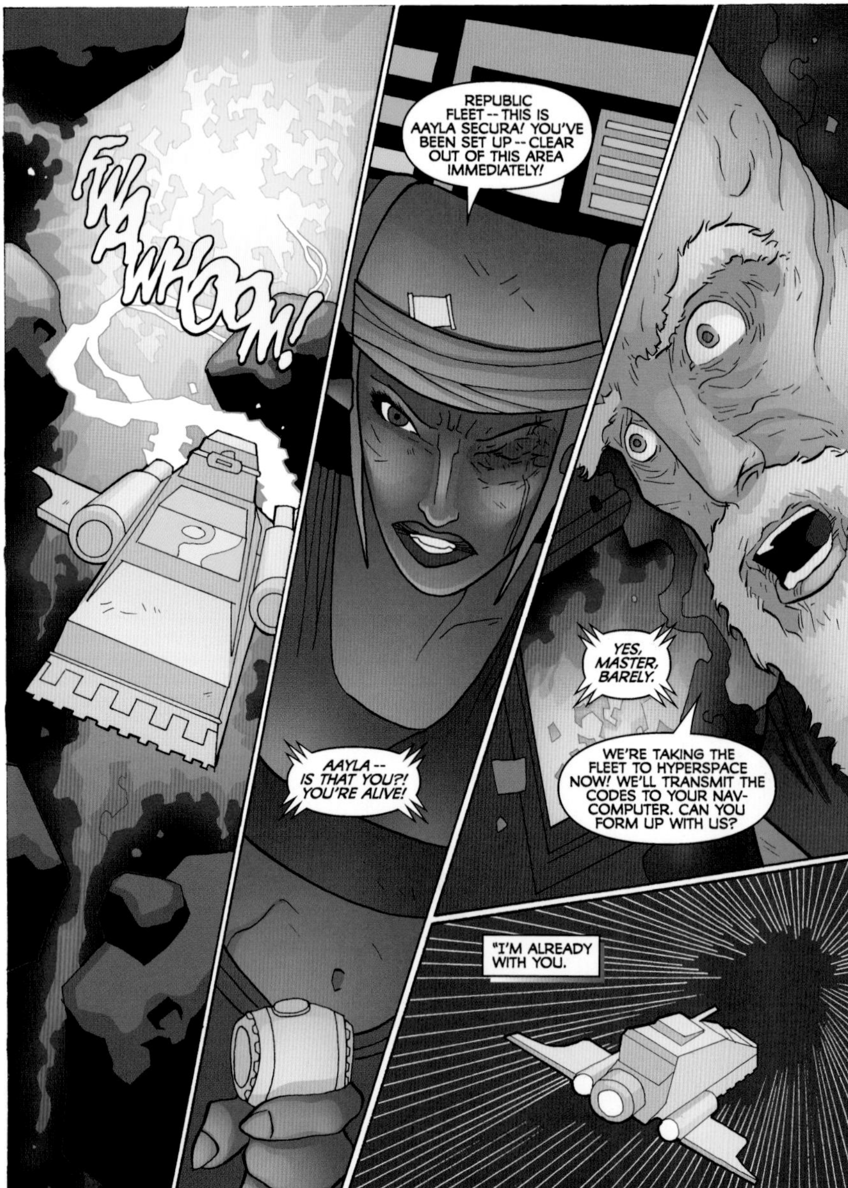
FWAWHOOM!
REPUBLIC FLEET -- THIS IS AAYLA SECURA! YOU'VE BEEN SET UP -- CLEAR OUT OF THIS AREA IMMEDIATELY!
AAYLA -- IS THAT YOU?! YOU'RE ALIVE!
YES, MASTER, BARELY.
WE'RE TAKING THE FLEET TO HYPERSPACE NOW! WE'LL TRANSMIT THE CODES TO YOUR NAV-COMPUTER. CAN YOU FORM UP WITH US?
"I'M ALREADY WITH YOU.

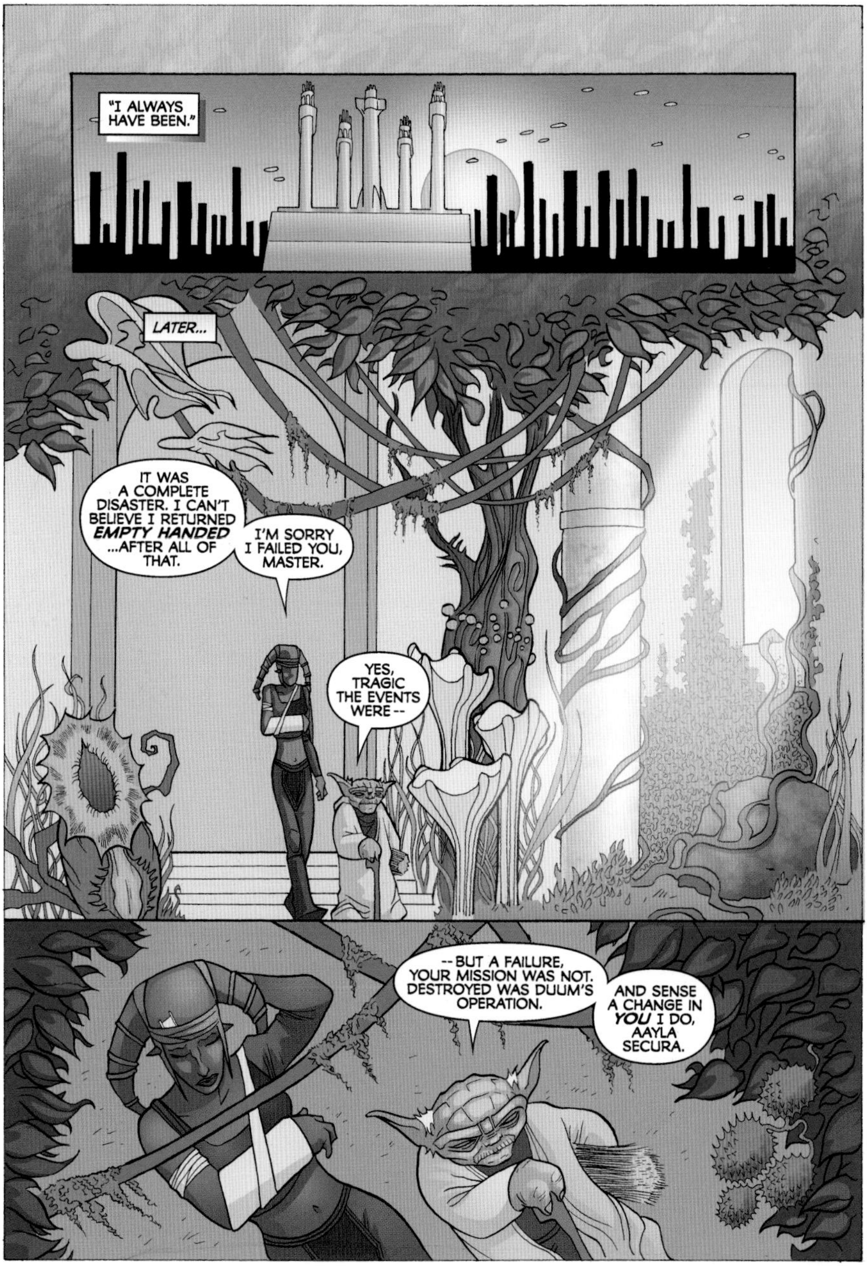
"I ALWAYS HAVE BEEN."
LATER...
IT WAS A COMPLETE DISASTER. I CAN'T BELIEVE I RETURNED EMPTY HANDED ...AFTER ALL OF THAT.
I'M SORRY I FAILED YOU, MASTER.
YES, TRAGIC THE EVENTS WERE--
--BUT A FAILURE, YOUR MISSION WAS NOT. DESTROYED WAS DUUM'S OPERATION.
AND SENSE A CHANGE IN YOU I DO, AAYLA SECURA.

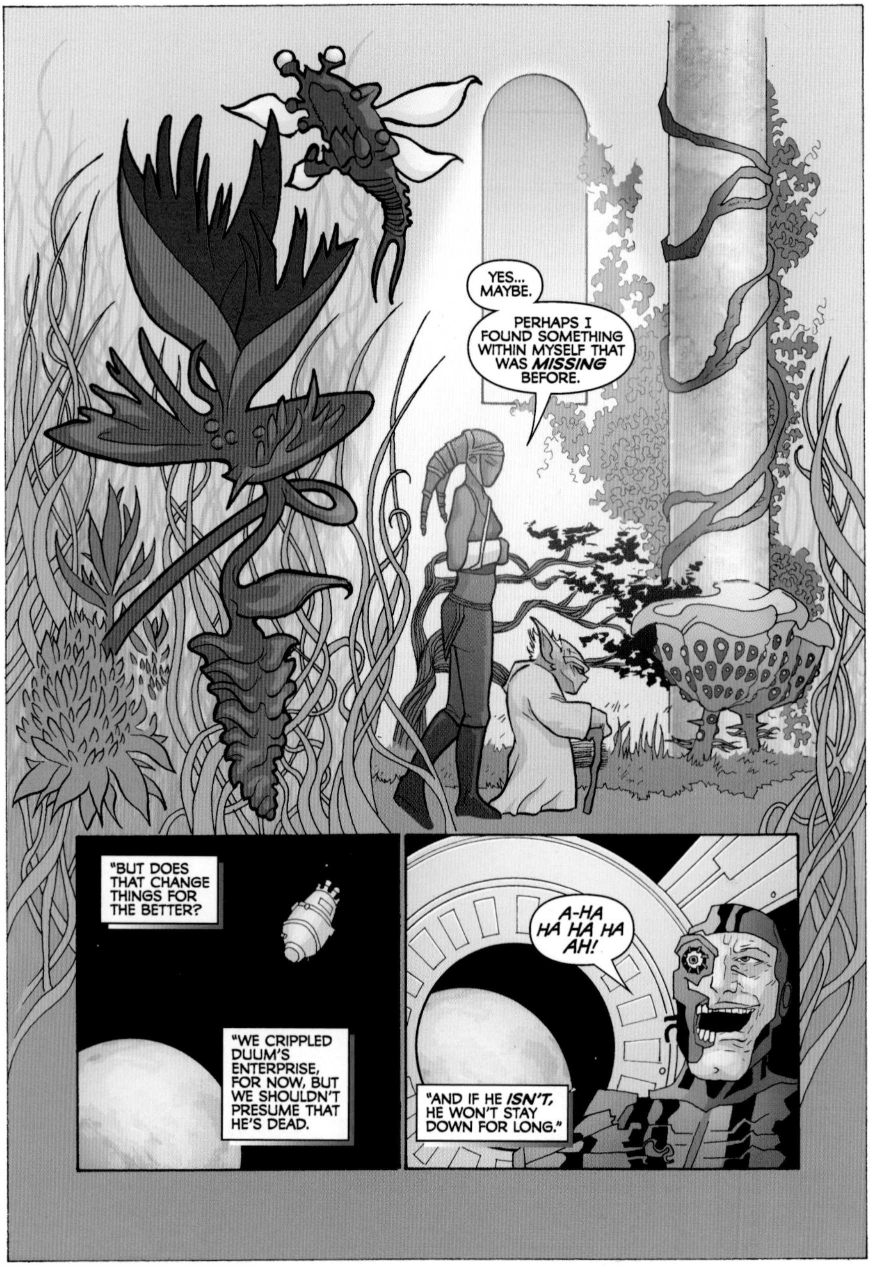
YES... MAYBE.
PERHAPS I FOUND SOMETHING WITHIN MYSELF THAT WAS *MISSING* BEFORE.
"BUT DOES THAT CHANGE THINGS FOR THE BETTER?
"WE CRIPPLED DUUM'S ENTERPRISE, FOR NOW, BUT WE SHOULDN'T PRESUME THAT HE'S DEAD.
A-HA HA HA HA AH!
"AND IF HE *ISN'T,* HE WON'T STAY DOWN FOR LONG."

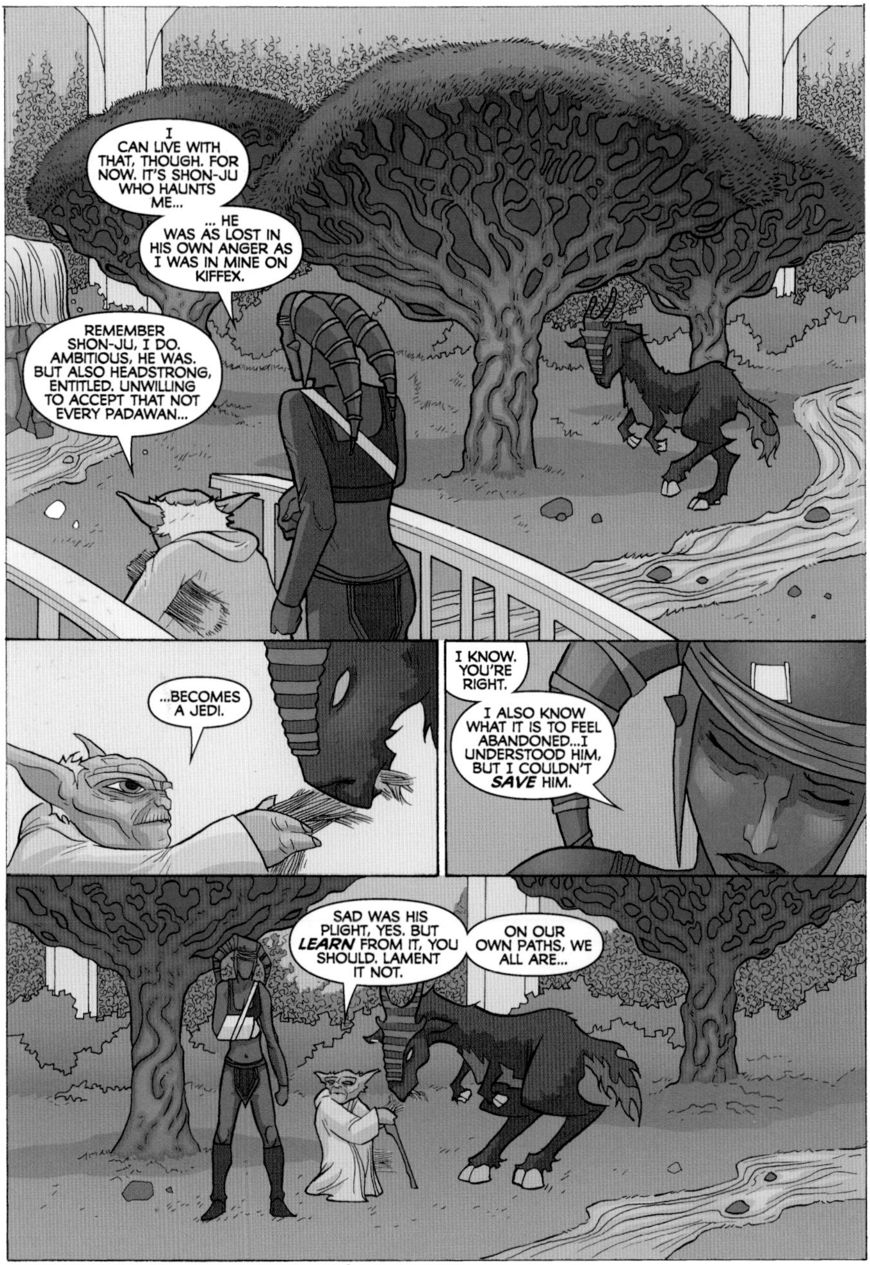
I CAN LIVE WITH THAT, THOUGH. FOR NOW. IT'S SHON-JU WHO HAUNTS ME...
... HE WAS AS LOST IN HIS OWN ANGER AS I WAS IN MINE ON KIFFEX.
REMEMBER SHON-JU, I DO. AMBITIOUS, HE WAS. BUT ALSO HEADSTRONG, ENTITLED. UNWILLING TO ACCEPT THAT NOT EVERY PADAWAN...
...BECOMES A JEDI.
I KNOW. YOU'RE RIGHT.
I ALSO KNOW WHAT IT IS TO FEEL ABANDONED...I UNDERSTOOD HIM, BUT I COULDN'T *SAVE* HIM.
SAD WAS HIS PLIGHT, YES. BUT *LEARN* FROM IT, YOU SHOULD. LAMENT IT NOT.
ON OUR OWN PATHS, WE ALL ARE...

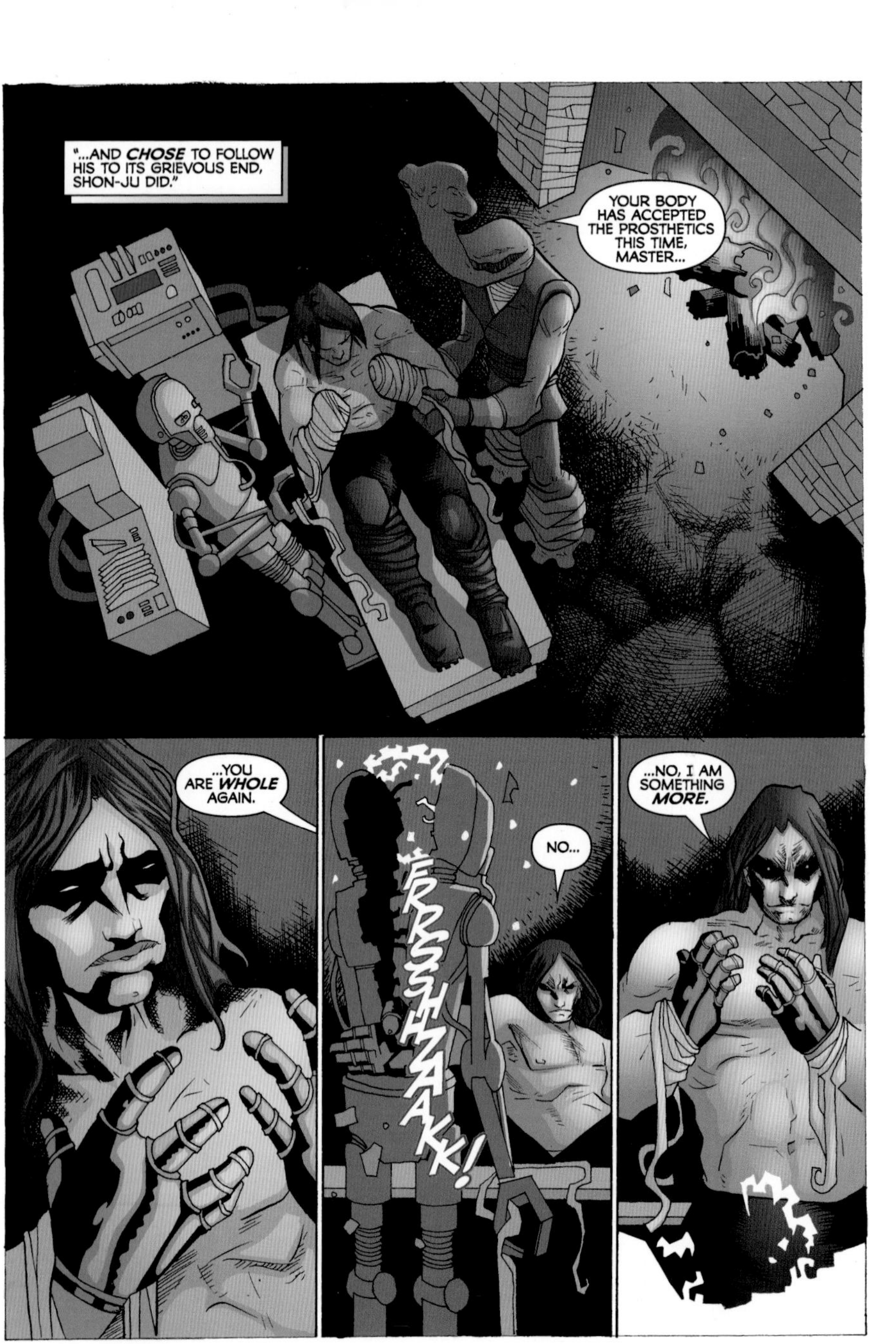
"...AND *CHOSE* TO FOLLOW HIS TO ITS GRIEVOUS END, SHON-JU DID."
YOUR BODY HAS ACCEPTED THE PROSTHETICS THIS TIME, MASTER...
...YOU ARE *WHOLE* AGAIN.
FRRSSHHZAKK!
NO...
...NO, I AM SOMETHING *MORE.*

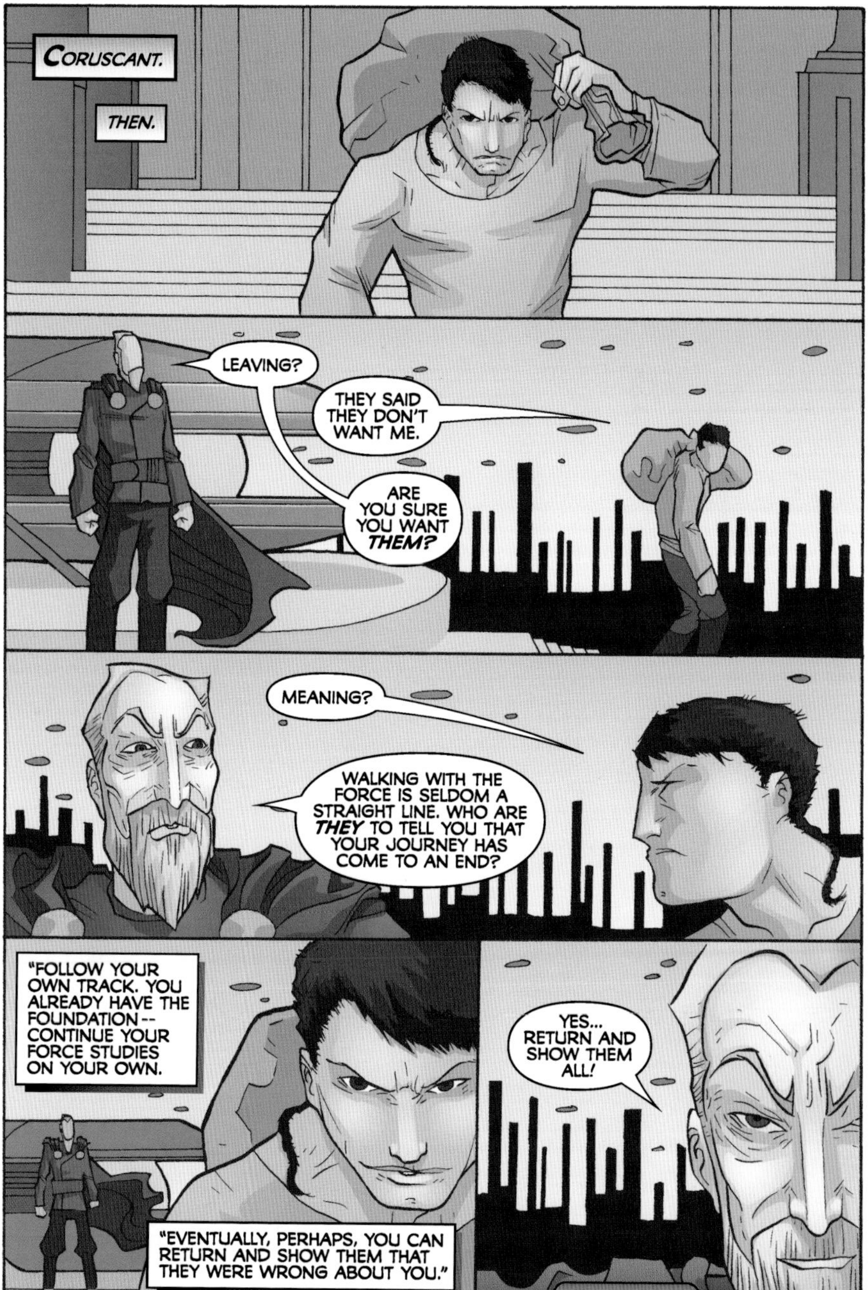
CORUSCANT.
THEN.
LEAVING?
THEY SAID THEY DON'T WANT ME.
ARE YOU SURE YOU WANT *THEM?*
MEANING?
WALKING WITH THE FORCE IS SELDOM A STRAIGHT LINE. WHO ARE *THEY* TO TELL YOU THAT YOUR JOURNEY HAS COME TO AN END?
"FOLLOW YOUR OWN TRACK. YOU ALREADY HAVE THE FOUNDATION-- CONTINUE YOUR FORCE STUDIES ON YOUR OWN.
"EVENTUALLY, PERHAPS, YOU CAN RETURN AND SHOW THEM THAT THEY WERE WRONG ABOUT YOU."
YES... RETURN AND SHOW THEM ALL!
THE END

STAR WARS GRAPHIC NOVEL TIMELINE (IN YEARS)

Omnibus: Tales of the Jedi—5,000–3,986 BSW4

Knights of the Old Republic—3,964–3,963 BSW4

The Old Republic—3653,3678 BSW4

Jedi vs. Sith—1,000 BSW4

Omnibus: Rise of the Sith—33 BSW4

Episode I: The Phantom Menace—32 BSW4

Omnibus: Emissaries and Assassins—32 BSW4

Twilight—31 BSW4

Bounty Hunters—31 BSW4

Omnibus: Menace Revealed—31–22 BSW4

Darkness—30 BSW4

The Stark Hyperspace War—30 BSW4

Rite of Passage—28 BSW4

Honor and Duty—24 BSW4

Episode II: Attack of the Clones—22 BSW4

Clone Wars—22–19 BSW4

Clone Wars Adventures—22–19 BSW4

General Grievous—22–19 BSW4

Episode III: Revenge of the Sith—19 BSW4

Dark Times—19 BSW4

Omnibus: Droids—5.5 BSW4

Boba Fett: Enemy of the Empire—3 BSW4

Underworld—1 BSW4

Episode IV: A New Hope—SW4

Classic Star Wars—0–3 ASW4

A Long Time Ago . . .—0–4 ASW4

Empire—0 ASW4

Rebellion—0 ASW4

Boba Fett: Man with a Mission—0 ASW4

Omnibus: Early Victories—0–3 ASW4

Jabba the Hutt: The Art of the Deal—1 ASW4

Episode V: The Empire Strikes Back—3 ASW4

Omnibus: Shadows of the Empire—3.5–4.5 ASW4

Episode VI: Return of the Jedi—4 ASW4

Omnibus: X-Wing Rogue Squadron—4–5 ASW4

Heir to the Empire—9 ASW4

Dark Force Rising—9 ASW4

The Last Command—9 ASW4

Dark Empire—10 ASW4

Boba Fett: Death, Lies, and Treachery—10 ASW4

Crimson Empire—11 ASW4

Jedi Academy: Leviathan—12 ASW4

Union—19 ASW4

Chewbacca—25 ASW4

Invasion—25 ASW4

Legacy—130–137 ASW4

Old Republic Era
25,000 – 1000 years before
Star Wars: A New Hope

Rise of the Empire Era
1000 – 0 years before
Star Wars: A New Hope

Rebellion Era
0 – 5 years after
Star Wars: A New Hope

New Republic Era
5 – 25 years after
Star Wars: A New Hope

New Jedi Order Era
25+ years after
Star Wars: A New Hope

Legacy Era
130+ years after
Star Wars: A New Hope

Infinities
Does not apply to timeline

Sergio Aragonés Stomps Star Wars
Star Wars Tales
Star Wars Infinities
Tag and Bink
Star Wars Visionaries

BSW4 = before *Episode IV: A New Hope*. ASW4 = after *Episode IV: A New Hope*.

FOR MORE ADVENTURE IN A GALAXY FAR, FAR, AWAY...

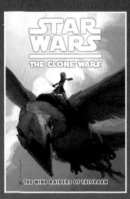
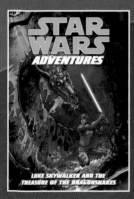

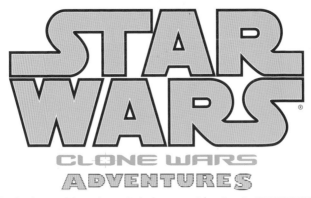
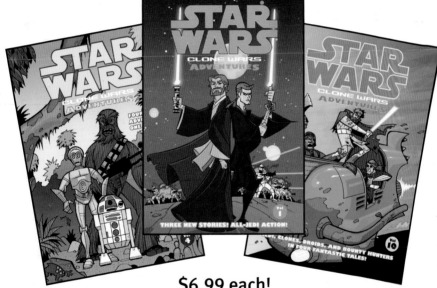